Welcome Home
SUPER SIMPLE
ENTERTAINING

FUSS-FREE MEALS FOR DINING IN WITH FRIENDS AND FAMILY

Hope Comerford

Good Books

New York, New York

Good Books books may be purchased in bulk at special discounts for sales promotion, corporate gifts, fund-raising, or educational purposes. Special editions can also be created to specifications. For details, contact the Special Sales Department, Good Books, 307 West 36th Street, 11th Floor, New York, NY 10018 or info@skyhorsepublishing.com.

Good Books is an imprint of Skyhorse Publishing, Inc.®, a Delaware corporation.

Visit our website at www.goodbooks.com.

10 9 8 7 6 5 4 3 2 1

Library of Congress Cataloging-in-Publication Data is available on file.

Cover design by Mona Lin
Cover photos by Meredith Special Interest Media

Print ISBN: 978-1-68099-623-4
Ebook ISBN: 978-1-68099-684-5

Printed in China

Table of Contents

About Welcome Home Super Simple Entertaining

We've put together 127 of the best simple recipes for entertaining for your Instant Pot, Slow Cooker, Stovetop, or Oven. Cooking for others can often be stressful. Worry no more! You've now got an arsenal of recipes you know you can trust! All of these recipes are easy to prepare, use common ingredients, and are delicious, of course. They're the perfect solution for when you're having family, friends, neighbors, or even co-workers over. There is truly something for every kind of gathering you might be having! This book even includes options for gluten-free, vegetarian, and plant-based cooking.

I always suggest reading cookbooks from cover to cover. I can't tell you the good recipes I've passed on by not following this advice. Bookmark or dog-ear the pages of the recipes that you think the guests you have coming over would enjoy the most, or that fit with their dietary needs. Then, when you've looked at everything, go back to those marked pages and narrow it down. Make yourself a grocery list and grab what you don't already have. Voilà! You're ready to get cooking! Entertaining guests has never been easier!

Safe Entertaining During a Pandemic

Inviting friends, family, neighbors, or strangers to share a meal these days feels different than it did before COVID-19. Many of us are more eager than ever to spend time with loved ones, and yet we're also more aware of the potential risks. Here are some tips for limiting the spread of germs while enjoying good food and quality time together.

- Whenever possible, gather outside rather than in your home.
- Invite one household or individual at a time, rather than hosting a large get-together with multiple families.
- Avoid common touch points as much as you can. Give each guest (or each household) their own dish of appetizers or other finger foods so that you're not all reaching your hands into the same dishes. You can also set out plates and silverware for each guest so that they're not grabbing from a common pile.
- Provide a hand washing station or hand sanitizer and have extra masks on hand for guests who may not bring their own.
- Consider setting up small tables with chairs at least six feet apart from each other, rather than having one big table for everyone.
- Be clear about your expectations when you invite guests, and be comfortable reminding people throughout the gathering. It may feel strange (after all, this is new territory for all of us), but with a little planning and practice it's possible to be gracious and safe at the same time!

Appetizers

Blackberry Baked Brie

Hope Comerford
Clinton Township, MI

Gluten-Free, Vegetarian

Makes 4–6 servings

Prep. Time: 5 minutes ⚜ *Cooking Time: 15 minutes* ⚜ *Setting: Manual* ⚜ *Pressure: High* ⚜ *Release: Manual*

8-oz. round Brie
1 cup water
¼ cup blackberry preserves
2 tsp. chopped fresh mint

Note from the cook:

I love to serve this at parties. It not only looks impressive, but it's so easy to throw together last minute.

1. Slice a grid pattern into the top of the rind of the Brie with a knife.

2. In a 7-inch round baking dish, place the Brie, then cover the baking dish securely with foil.

3. Insert the trivet into the inner pot of the Instant Pot; pour in the water.

4. Make a foil sling and arrange it on top of the trivet. Place the baking dish on top of the trivet and foil sling.

5. Secure the lid to the locked position and turn the vent to sealing.

6. Press Manual set the Instant Pot for 15 minutes on high pressure.

7. When cooking time is up, turn off the Instant Pot and do a quick release of the pressure.

8. When the valve has dropped, remove the lid, then remove the baking dish.

9. Remove the top rind of the Brie and top with the preserves. Sprinkle with the fresh mint.

Serving suggestion:

Serve with crostini, baguettes, or crackers. (Rice crackers are my favorite with this.)

Zesty and Fruity Cream Cheese Block

Hope Comerford
Clinton Township, MI

*Gluten-Free, Vegetarian

Makes 1 cup

Prep. Time: 5 minutes ⅙ Cooking Time: 8–10 minutes ⅙ Cooling Time: 10–15 minutes

2 tsp. olive oil

¼ cup minced shallot or onion

1–2 chipotle peppers in adobo sauce (depending on the level of heat you like), minced

1 cup strawberry preserves (or any other flavor you like)

8-oz. block cream cheese

rice crackers or other crisp crackers

*Recipe Note:

To make this recipe gluten-free, be sure you choose a brand of chipotles in adobo sauce that are gluten-free.

1. In a small sauté pan, heat the oil over medium heat.

2. Sauté the shallots and chipotle peppers until the shallots are translucent. Add the strawberry preserves and heat until the mixture has thickened.

3. Let the preserves mixture cool for about 10–15 minutes.

4. Place the cream cheese block on a serving plate or platter and pour the preserves mixture over the top.

5. Serve with crisp crackers, such as rice crackers.

Guacamole

Kara Maddox
Lincoln, NE
Judy Houser
Hershey, PA

*Gluten-Free, Vegetarian, Plant-Based

Makes about 1¼–2 cups

Prep. Time: 10 minutes

2 avocados
½ cup chopped red onion
½ cup cubed tomatoes
salt and pepper to taste
I tsp. lime juice

1. Cut the avocados in half, remove the stone, and peel. Then mash the avocados in a medium-sized mixing bowl with a fork.

2. Stir in remaining ingredients gently.

3. Serve with cut-up fresh vegetables and corn chips.

Easy Layered Taco Dip

QUICK & EASY

Lindsey Spencer
Morrow, OH
Jenny R. Unternahrer
Wayland, IA

Gluten-Free, Vegetarian, Plant-Based option

Makes 8–10 servings

Prep. Time: 15 minutes

8-oz. cream cheese, softened

8-oz. sour cream

8-oz. taco sauce or salsa

shredded lettuce

chopped tomato

chopped green pepper, optional

shredded cheese, cheddar or Mexican blend

tortilla chips

1. Blend cream cheese and sour cream until smooth.

2. Spread in bottom of a 9×13-inch dish.

3. Layer salsa over sour cream mixture, then lettuce, tomato, green pepper (if using), and cheese.

4. Serve with tortilla chips.

*Recipe Notes:

To make this recipe gluten-free, be sure to choose a taco sauce or salsa that is gluten-free.

To make this recipe plant-based, choose a vegan cream cheese, sour cream, salsa, and vegan shredded cheese.

Variations:

1. Instead of salsa, use 1-oz. packet of taco seasoning to mix with the cream cheese and sour cream.

　　　　　—Virginia Graybill, Hershey, PA

2. Add a layer of chopped onion.

　　　　　—Barbara J. Bey, Hillsboro, OH

Tip:

If you can, add the lettuce, tomato, and cheese at the last minute so the lettuce doesn't get soggy.

　　　　　—Jenny R. Unternahrer, Wayland, IA

Feta Bruschetta

Lena Sheaffer
Port Matilda, PA

*Gluten-Free option, Vegetarian, Plant-Based option

Makes 10 servings

Prep. Time: 15 minutes ⚬ Baking Time: 20 minutes

4 Tbsp. butter, melted

1¼ cups olive or vegetable oil

10 slices French bread, cut 1-inch thick

4-oz. pkg. crumbled feta cheese

2–3 cloves garlic, minced

1 Tbsp. chopped fresh basil, or 1 tsp. dried basil

1 large tomato, seeded and chopped

1. Combine butter and oil. Brush on both sides of bread. Place on baking sheet.

2. Bake at 350°F for 8–10 minutes, or until lightly browned.

3. Combine feta cheese, garlic, and basil. Sprinkle over toast. Top with tomato.

4. Bake 8–10 minutes longer, or until heated through. Serve warm.

*Recipe Notes:

To make this recipe gluten-free, swap out the French bread for gluten-free bread.

To make this recipe plant-based, swap out butter for vegan butter or coconut oil, choose olive oil over vegetable oil, use a vegan bread, and use vegan feta cheese.

Variation:

Mix chopped red pepper into Step 3, along with any of your other favorite herbs.

Party Pinwheels

Della Yoder
Kalona, IA

*Vegetarian

Makes 36 pieces

Prep. Time: 20–25 minutes ⚜ *Chilling Time: 2 hours*

1-oz. packet Original Hidden Valley
Ranch Dressing Mix

2 (8-oz.) pkgs. cream cheese, softened

2 green onions, minced

4 (12-inch) flour tortillas

4-oz. jar diced pimentos, drained

4-oz. can diced green chilies, drained

2¼-oz. can diced black olives, drained

1. Mix together ranch mix, cream cheese, and green onions. Spread onto tortillas.

2. Sprinkle equal amounts of vegetables over cream cheese mixture.

3. Roll up tortillas tightly. Refrigerate for at least 2 hours.

4. Cut tortillas into 1-inch slices. Discard ends. Serve with spirals facing up.

Stuffed Mushrooms

Doris Herr
Manheim, PA

*Vegetarian

Makes 18 mushrooms, or 9 servings

Prep. Time: 30 minutes   Cooking/Baking Time: 25 minutes

18 medium-sized mushrooms
1 stick (¼ lb.) butter, melted
¼ cup chopped onions
¼ cup chopped celery
1 cup dry cornbread stuffing
¼ cup water

1. Wash mushrooms. Carefully remove stems. Set stems aside.

2. Lightly grease a shallow 7×11-inch baking dish.

3. Melt butter in a small skillet. Dip mushroom caps into melted butter in skillet. Place upside down in prepared baking dish.

4. Chop ½ cup mushroom stems. Place in butter in skillet, along with chopped celery and onion. Sauté in butter.

5. Mix stuffing crumbs with water in a small bowl. Add to vegetables in skillet and stir.

6. Spoon mixture into mushroom caps.

7. Bake at 350°F for 25 minutes.

Variations:

1. Use flavored stuffing instead of the cornbread stuffing.
2. Replace celery with crumbled blue cheese.

—Lena Stauffer
Port Matilda, PA

Stuffed Jalapeños

Barbara Walker
Sturgis, SD

*Gluten-Free option

Makes 12 servings

Prep. Time: 20 minutes   ♣   Cooking/Baking Time: 45 minutes

12 fresh jalapeño peppers, halved
lengthwise and seeded

8-oz. pkg. cream cheese, softened

12 slices bacon

*Recipe Note:
To make this recipe gluten-free,
choose gluten-free bacon.

1. Preheat oven to 400°F.

2. Use rubber gloves to seed and slice peppers. Keep hands away from your face; the liquid and seeds from the peppers can burn your eyes.

3. Stuff each pepper half with cream cheese.

4. Wrap half a slice of bacon around each stuffed pepper.

5. Place in single layer on baking sheet.

6. Bake for 45 minutes, or until bacon is done.

Root Beer Chicken Wings

Hope Comerford
Clinton Township, MI

Gluten-Free

Makes 15–18 servings

Prep. Time: 2 minutes   Cooking Time: 18 minutes   Setting: Manual
Pressure: High   Release: Manual

5 lb. chicken wings, tips removed and separated at joint

12-oz. can plus ¼ cup root beer, divided

¼ cup brown sugar

½ tsp. red pepper flakes

1. Place all the chicken wing pieces into the inner pot of the Instant Pot. Pour the can of root beer over the top.

2. Secure the lid and turn the vent to sealing.

3. Press Manual and set the Instant Pot to 18 minutes on high pressure.

4. Preheat the oven on broil.

5. When cooking time is up, turn off the Instant Pot and do a quick release of the pressure.

6. Remove the wings and spread them out on a baking sheet.

7. Mix together the ¼ cup root beer, brown sugar, and red pepper flakes. Brush this over the wings.

8. Place the wings under the broiler for 2 minutes.

Bacon-Wrapped Water Chestnuts

John D. Allen
Rye, CO

*Gluten-Free option

Makes 10–12 servings

Marinating Time: 1 hour ❧ Prep. Time: 45 minutes ❧ Cooking/Baking Time: 30 minutes

8-oz. can water chestnuts, drained
¼ cup soy sauce
1 lb. bacon
½ cup brown sugar

1. Soak the water chestnuts in soy sauce for 1 hour.

2. Cut the bacon in half crosswise. Fry until limp but not crisp.

3. Roll the chestnuts in brown sugar.

4. Wrap bacon around the chestnuts and secure with toothpicks. Place on a baking sheet.

5. Bake at 350°F for 30 minutes.

*Recipe Note:
To make this recipe gluten-free, use tamari soy sauce or liquid aminos instead of soy sauce and choose a gluten-free bacon.

Soups, Stews & Chilies

Meatball Tortellini Soup

Lucille Amos
Greensboro, NC

Vegetarian Option

Makes 4 servings

Prep. Time: 5 minutes ⚬ *Cooking Time: 20–25 minutes*

14-oz. can beef broth
12 frozen Italian meatballs
1 cup stewed tomatoes
11-oz. can Mexi-corn, drained
1 cup frozen cheese tortellini

1. Bring broth to boil in a large stockpot

2. Add meatballs. Cover and reduce heat. Simmer 5 minutes.

3. Add tomatoes and corn. Cover and simmer 5 minutes more.

4. Add tortellini. Cover and simmer 5 more minutes, or until tortellini is tender.

*Recipe Note:

To make this recipe vegetarian, swap the beef broth for vegetable broth and swap the Italian meatballs for meatless meatballs.

Stuffed Sweet Pepper Soup

STOVETOP

Moreen Weaver
Bath, NY

*Gluten-Free option, Vegetarian option, Plant-Based option

Makes 10 servings

Prep. Time: 20 minutes & Cooking Time: 1 hour

I lb. 95%-lean ground beef
2 qts. low-sodium tomato juice
3 medium red, or green, bell peppers, diced
1½ cups chili sauce, no salt added
I cup uncooked brown rice
2 celery ribs, diced
I large onion, diced
3 low-sodium chicken bouillon cubes
2 cloves garlic, minced

1. In large kettle over medium heat, cook beef until no longer pink. Drain off drippings.

2. Add remaining ingredients. Bring to a boil.

3. Reduce heat. Simmer, uncovered, for 1 hour, or until rice is tender.

*Recipe Notes:

To make this recipe gluten-free, choose a gluten-free chili sauce and choose gluten-free chicken bouillon cubes.

To make this recipe vegetarian and/or plant-based, swap the ground beef for meatless crumbles, or use beans instead and swap the chicken bouillon cubes for vegetable bouillon cubes.

Quick and Easy Chili

Carolyn Spohn
Shawnee, KS

*Gluten-Free option, Vegetarian option, Plant-Based option

Makes 3–4 servings

Prep. Time: 10 minutes ❧ Cooking Time: 25 minutes

½ lb. ground beef, or turkey, browned and drained

1 medium-sized onion, chopped

2 cloves garlic, minced

2 (15-oz.) cans chili-style beans with liquid

8-oz. can tomato sauce

*Recipe Notes:

To make this gluten-free, choose gluten-free chili style beans.

To make this vegetarian and/or plant-based, swap the ground beef/turkey for meatless crumbles.

1. Brown ground beef in a large skillet.

2. Drain, leaving about 1 tsp. drippings in pan. Sauté onions and garlic until softened.

3. Add beans, with liquid, and the tomato sauce. Bring to a slow boil.

4. Reduce heat to simmer and cook for 15 minutes.

5. Return meat to skillet. Heat together for 5 minutes.

Tip:
Leftovers makes good chili dogs.

Italian Pasta Soup

Sharon Timpe
Jackson, WI

*Gluten-Free option, Vegetarian option, Plant-Based option

Makes 6 servings

Prep. Time: 10–15 minutes   Cooking Time: 30 minutes

2 (14½-oz.) cans chicken broth

1 cup water

1 cup uncooked elbow macaroni

18 frozen Italian-style, or regular, meatballs

2 cups fresh spinach leaves, finely shredded

8-oz. can pizza sauce

1. In a large stockpot, bring broth and water to a boil.

2. Add pasta and meatballs and return to a boil. Lower heat and continue cooking 8 to 10 minutes, or until pasta is done and meatballs are hot. Stir occasionally. Do not drain.

3. Add spinach and pizza sauce. Simmer 2 minutes, or until heated thoroughly.

*Recipe Notes:

To make this recipe gluten-free, choose a gluten-free chicken broth, gluten-free pasta, gluten-free meatballs, and gluten-free pizza sauce.

To make this recipe vegetarian and/or plant-based, swap the chicken broth with vegetable broth and swap the meatballs for meatless meatballs.

Chunky Beef Chili

Ruth C. Hancock
Earlsboro, OK

*Gluten-Free option

Makes 4 servings

Prep. Time: 30 minutes ⚬ *Cooking Time: 1¾–2¼ hours*

2 Tbsp. vegetable oil, divided

1 lb. beef stew, cut into 1½-inch thick pieces

1 medium onion, chopped

1 medium jalapeño pepper with seeds, minced, optional

½ tsp. salt

2 (14½-oz.) cans chili-seasoned diced tomatoes

*Recipe Note:

To make this gluten-free, choose gluten-free chili-seasoned tomatoes, or just used regular diced tomatoes and add a teaspoon of chili powder.

1. Heat 1 Tbsp. oil in stockpot over medium heat until hot.

2. Brown half of beef in oil. Remove meat from pot and keep warm.

3. Repeat with remaining beef. Remove meat from pot and keep warm.

4. Add remaining 1 Tbsp. oil to stockpot, along with the onion, and the pepper if you wish.

5. Cook 5–8 minutes, or until vegetables are tender. Stir occasionally.

6. Return meat and juices to stockpot. Add salt and tomatoes.

7. Bring to a boil. Reduce heat. Cover tightly and simmer 1¾–2¼ hours, or until meat is tender but not dried out.

Beef Barley Soup

Stacie Skelly
Millersville, PA

Makes 8–10 servings

Prep. Time: 15 minutes   ❧   Cooking Time: 9¼–11½ hours   ❧   Ideal slow-cooker size: 6-qt.

3–4-lb. chuck roast

2 cups carrots, chopped

6 cups low-sodium vegetable
or tomato juice, divided

2 cups quick-cook barley

water, to desired consistency

salt and pepper to taste, optional

1. Place roast, carrots, and 4 cups juice in the slow cooker.

2. Cover and cook on Low 8–10 hours.

3. Remove roast. Place on platter and cover with foil to keep warm.

4. Meanwhile, add barley to the slow cooker. Stir well. Turn heat to High and cook 45 minutes to 1 hour, until barley is tender.

5. While barley is cooking, cut meat into bite-sized pieces.

6. When barley is tender, return chopped beef to the slow cooker. Add 2 cups juice, water if you wish, and salt and pepper, if you want. Cook for 30 minutes on High, or until soup is heated through.

Roast Beef Stew

Thelma Good
Harrisonburg, VA

*Gluten-Free

Makes 8 servings

Prep. Time: 10–15 minutes ❧ Cooking Time: 8–11 hours ❧ Ideal slow-cooker size: 6-qt.

2–3-lb. roast
5–6 potatoes, quartered
4–5 carrots, sliced
2 small onions, sliced
half a head of cabbage, sliced

1. Place roast in crock.

2. Cover and cook on Low for 6–8 hours.

3. Place the potatoes, carrots, and onions around and over the roast. Fill slow cooker ½–¾ full with water, depending upon how soupy you like your stew.

4. Cover and cook on High 2–3 hours.

5. Lift the lid and put in the cabbage, pushing it down into the broth. Continue cooking on High 1 more hour, or until veggies are done to your liking. The stew should be ready at lunchtime—or dinnertime.

Variations:

1. Sprinkle the roast, top and bottom, with salt and pepper before placing it in the cooker in Step 1. Also, sprinkle the vegetables with salt after you've put them in the cooker in Step 3.

2. Increase the amount of potatoes, carrots, onions, and cabbage to your liking. You may need to increase the cooking time in Steps 4 and 5 to make sure that they get as tender as you like.

Baked Potato Soup

Flo Quint
Quinter, KS

Susan Nafziger
Canton, KS

Gluten-Free option, Vegetarian, Plant-Based option

Makes 6–8 servings

Prep. Time: 30 minutes & Cooking Time: 15–20 minutes

1½ sticks (12 Tbsp.) butter

⅔ cup flour

7 cups milk

4 cups baked potatoes (about 5 large potatoes), peeled and cubed

4 green onions, sliced thin

8–12 strips bacon (according to your taste preference), cooked and crumbled

1¼ cups shredded cheese

8 oz. sour cream, optional

¾ tsp. salt, optional

¼ tsp. pepper, optional

1. Melt butter in large stockpot. Add flour and stir until smooth over medium heat.

2. Add milk, stirring often until thickened. Be careful not to scorch.

3. Add potatoes and onions and bring to a boil. Reduce heat and simmer 5 minutes, stirring often.

4. Remove from heat and add bacon, cheese, and sour cream if desired. Stir until melted.

5. Add seasonings if desired and blend thoroughly.

Variation:

Instead of 7 cups milk, you can use 4 cups milk and 3 cups chicken broth.

*Recipe Notes:

To make this recipe gluten-free swap the flour for gluten-free flour blend.

To make this recipe plant-based, swap the butter for vegan butter, swap the shredded cheese for vegan shredded cheese, and swap the sour cream for vegan sour cream.

Quickie French Onion Soup

Mary Puskar
Forest Hill, MD

*Gluten-Free Option, Vegetarian option

Makes 6–8 servings

Prep. Time: 5–10 minutes ⚬ Cooking Time: 1 hour

half a stick (¼ cup) butter

3–4 good-sized onions (enough to make 5 cups sliced onions)

¼ cup flour

6 cups beef broth, or 3 (14½-oz.) cans beef broth, or 6 cups water with 6 beef bouillon cubes

6–8 melba rounds, optional

2 cups grated mozzarella cheese, optional

*Recipe Notes:

To make this gluten-free, choose a gluten-free flour blend and choose gluten-free beef broth. Skip the melba rounds.

To make this vegetarian, swap the beef broth for vegetable broth.

1. Melt butter in a large saucepan.

2. Meanwhile, slice onions.

3. Sauté onions in butter. After they become tender, continue cooking over low heat so that they brown and deepen in flavor, up to 30 minutes.

4. Sprinkle with flour. Cook 2 minutes.

5. Stir in broth, or water and bouillon cubes. Cover.

6. Heat to boiling and simmer 20 minutes.

7. Ladle into individual serving bowls.

8. Top each with melba rounds and/or grated cheese if you wish. For extra beauty and flavor, broil until cheese melts, but first make sure that the soup bowls can withstand the broiler heat. They could crack.

Navy Bean and Ham Soup

SLOW-COOKER

Jennifer Freed
Rockingham, VA

*Gluten-Free

Makes 6 servings

Prep. Time: overnight, or approximately 8 hours 🍃 Cooking Time: 8–10 hours
Ideal slow-cooker size: 6½- or 7-qt.

6 cups water

5 cups dried navy beans, soaked overnight, drained, and rinsed

1 pound ham, cubed

15-oz. can corn, drained

4-oz. can mild diced green chilies, drained

1 onion, diced, optional

salt and pepper to taste

1. Place all ingredients in the slow cooker.

2. Cover and cook on Low 8–10 hours, or until beans are tender.

Chicken Rice Soup

SLOW-COOKER

Norma Grieser
Clarksville, MI

*Gluten-Free option

Makes 8 servings

Prep. Time: 30 minutes ❧ *Cooking Time: 4–8 hours* ❧ *Ideal slow-cooker size: 4- to 6-qt.*

4 cups gluten-free low-sodium chicken broth

4 cups cut-up chicken, cooked

1⅓ cups cut-up celery

1⅓ cups diced carrots

1 qt. water

1 cup uncooked long-grain rice

1. Put all ingredients in the slow cooker.

2. Cover and cook on Low 4–8 hours, or until vegetables are cooked to your liking.

*Recipe Note:
To make this recipe gluten-free, choose a gluten-free chicken broth.

Easy Chicken Tortilla Soup

SLOW-COOKER

Becky Harder
Monument, CO

Gluten-Free, Vegetarian option, Plant-Based option

Makes 6–8 servings

Prep. Time: 5–10 minutes ❧ *Cooking Time: 8 hours* ❧ *Ideal slow-cooker size: 4- to 5-qt.*

4 chicken breast halves

2 (15-oz.) cans black beans, undrained

2 (15-oz.) cans Mexican stewed tomatoes, or Ro*Tel tomatoes

1 cup salsa (mild, medium, or hot, whichever you prefer)

4-oz. can chopped green chilies

14½-oz. can tomato sauce

tortilla chips

1. Combine all ingredients in large slow cooker.

2. Cover. Cook on Low 8 hours.

3. Just before serving, remove chicken breasts and slice into bite-sized pieces. Stir into soup.

4. Put a handful of tortilla chips in each individual soup bowl. Ladle soup over chips. Top with shredded cheese.

*Recipe Notes:

To make this gluten-free, choose gluten-free Mexican stewed tomatoes and choose gluten-free salsa.

To make this vegetarian and/or plant-based, leave out the chicken. Add an extra can of black beans or use tofu in place of the chicken. Cook time will be reduced to 3–4 hours.

White Chicken Chili

Lucille Hollinger
Richland, PA

*Gluten-Free option

Makes 8 servings

Prep. Time: 10 minutes & Cooking Time: 5–6 hours & Ideal slow-cooker size: 3-qt.

4 cups cubed cooked chicken
2 cups chicken broth
2 (14½-oz.) cans cannellini beans
14½-oz. can garbanzo beans
1 cup shredded white cheddar cheese
¼ cup chopped onion
¼ cup chopped bell pepper
2 tsp. ground cumin
½ tsp. dried oregano
¼ tsp. cayenne pepper
¼ tsp. salt

*Recipe Note:
To make this recipe gluten-free, choose a gluten-free chicken broth.

1. Combine all ingredients in slow cooker.

2. Cover and cook on Low for 5–6 hours.

Variations:

Omit garbanzo beans. Shred chicken instead of cubing it. Add 1 tsp. Italian herb seasoning.

—Beverly Hummel

Serving suggestions:

Cornbread and salad.
Serve with sour cream, shredded cheese, and tortilla chips.

Creamy Broccoli Soup

SuAnne Burkholder
Millersburg, OH

*Gluten-Free Option

Makes 3–4 servings

Prep. Time: 10–15 minutes   *Cooking/Baking Time: 15–20 minutes*

4 cups milk, divided
2 Tbsp. cornstarch
1½ cups cut-up broccoli
1 Tbsp. chicken-flavored soup base
salt to taste

1. Heat 3 cups milk and chicken base in a stockpot over low heat until hot.

2. Meanwhile, place cut-up broccoli in a microwave-safe dish. Add 1 Tbsp. water. Cover. Microwave on High for 1½ minutes. Stir. Repeat until broccoli becomes bright green and just-tender. Be careful not to overcook it! Drain broccoli of liquid.

3. In a small bowl, or in a jar with a tight-fitting lid, mix together 1 cup milk and cornstarch until smooth. Slowly add to hot milk mixture.

4. Simmer gently, stirring constantly. When slightly thickened, add broccoli and salt.

*Recipe Note:
To make this recipe gluten-free, choose a gluten-free chicken-flavored soup base.

Main Dishes

Beef

Hearty Pot Roast

Colleen Heatwole
Burton, MI

*Gluten-Free option

Makes 12 servings, about 1 cup per serving

Prep. Time: 30 minutes ❧ Roasting Time: 2–2½ hours ❧ Standing Time: 10 minutes

4-lb. beef roast, ideally rump roast
4 medium red potatoes, cut in thirds
3 medium carrots, quartered
2 ribs celery, chopped
2 medium onions, sliced
½ cup flour
6-oz. can tomato paste
¼ cup water
1 tsp. instant beef bouillon, or 1 beef bouillon cube
¼ tsp. pepper

*Recipe Notes:

To make this recipe gluten-free, swap the flour for a gluten-free flour blend and choose gluten-free beef bouillon.

1. Place roast in 9×13-inch baking pan or roaster.

2. Arrange vegetables around roast.

3. Combine flour, tomato paste, water, bouillon, and pepper in small bowl.

4. Pour over meat and vegetables.

5. Cover. Roast at 325°F for 2–2½ hours, or until meat thermometer registers 170°F.

6. Allow meat to stand for 10 minutes.

7. Slice and place on platter surrounded by vegetables.

8. Pour gravy over top. Place additional gravy in bowl and serve along with platter.

Variation:

You can make this in a large oven cooking bag. Combine flour, tomato paste, water, bouillon, and pepper in a bowl. Pour into cooking bag. Place in 9×13-inch baking pan. Add roast to bag in pan. Add vegetables around roast in bag. Close bag with its tie. Make six ½-inch slits on top of bag. Roast according to instructions in Step 5 and following.

Coca-Cola Roast

Hope Comerford
Clinton Township, MI

*Gluten-Free

Makes 6 servings

Prep. Time: 10 minutes & *Cooking Time: 8–10 hours* & *Ideal slow-cooker size: 6-qt.*

3–4 lb. boneless bottom round steak

5–6 small potatoes, cut up if you'd like

4–5 medium-sized carrots peeled, cut in half or thirds

2–3 cloves garlic, chopped

salt to taste

pepper to taste

12-oz. can Coca-Cola

1. Place roast in crock.

2. Place potatoes and carrots around roast.

3. Sprinkle roast and veggies with the garlic, salt, and pepper.

4. Pour the can of Coca-Cola over the top.

5. Cover and cook on Low for 8–10 hours.

Pepper Steak

Darlene G. Martin
Richfield, PA

*Gluten-Free

Makes 4 servings

Prep. Time: 15–20 minutes ⚶ *Cooking Time: 5–6 hours* ⚶ *Ideal slow-cooker size: 3½- to 4-qt.*

1-lb. round steak, cut ¾–1-inch thick

14½-oz. can Italian-style stewed tomatoes, undrained

1 tsp. gluten-free Worcestershire sauce

2 yellow, 2 red, and 2 green bell peppers, sliced in strips

large onion, sliced

1. Cut meat into 4 serving-sized pieces. In a large nonstick skillet, brown meat on both sides. Transfer meat to a 3½- or 4-qt. slow cooker.

2. In medium bowl, stir together undrained tomatoes and Worcestershire sauce. Spoon over meat.

3. Arrange vegetables over top.

4. Cover and cook on Low 5–6 hours or until meat and vegetables are tender but not overcooked.

Veggie and Beef Stir Fry

Margaret H. Moffitt
Middleton, TN

Gluten-Free option

Makes 4 servings

Prep. Time: 15–20 minutes ⚬ *Cooking Time: 30–35 minutes*

¼ lb. beef tenderloin

2 tsp. olive oil

1 onion, chopped coarsely

1 small zucchini, chopped coarsely

3 cups coarsely chopped broccoli florets

½ a small yellow squash, chopped coarsely

½ cup uncooked brown rice

1 cup water

1 tsp. low-sodium teriyaki sauce

*Recipe Note:

To make this recipe gluten-free, choose a gluten-free teriyaki sauce.

1. Cut beef into ¼-inch-wide strips.

2. In a good-sized skillet, stir-fry beef in 2 tsp. olive oil just until no longer pink, about 2 minutes.

3. Add onion and other vegetables. Stir-fry until tender-crisp, about 5–7 minutes.

4. To cook rice, place rice and water in a saucepan. Cover, and bring to a boil. Adjust heat so that mixture simmers, covered. Cook rice until tender, about 20–25 minutes.

5. Just before serving over rice, add teriyaki sauce to beef and vegetables.

Herby French Dip Sandwiches

Sara Wichert
Hillsboro, KS

Gluten-Free

Makes 6–8 servings

Prep. Time: 5 minutes ⚘ *Cooking Time: 5–6 hours* ⚘ *Ideal slow-cooker size: 4-qt.*

3-lb. chuck roast

2 cups water

½ cup gluten-free, low-sodium soy sauce or liquid aminos

1 tsp. garlic powder

1 bay leaf

3–4 whole peppercorns

1 tsp. dried rosemary, optional

1 tsp. dried thyme, optional

1. Place roast in the slow cooker.

2. Combine remaining ingredients in a mixing bowl. Pour over meat.

3. Cover and cook on High 5–6 hours, or until meat is tender but not dry.

4. Remove meat from broth and shred with fork. Stir back into sauce.

5. Remove meat from the cooker by large forkfuls.

Serving suggestion:
Serve on French rolls or gluten-free rolls.

Chili-Lime Mexican Shredded Beef

Genelle Taylor
Perrysburg, OH

*Gluten-Free

Makes 6–8 servings

Prep. Time: 10 minutes ⚹ Cooking Time: 8 hours ⚹ Ideal slow-cooker size: 5- to 6-qt.

2–3-lb. beef chuck roast
4 cups lemon-lime soda
1 tsp. chili powder
1 tsp. salt
3 cloves garlic, crushed
2 limes, juiced

1. Place the roast in slow cooker.

2. Pour soda over roast.

3. Season with chili powder, salt, and garlic.

4. Cover and cook on Low for 8 hours.

5. Shred the beef, return to crock, pour lime juice over, and stir.

Serving suggestion:

Serve hot, with black beans and rice, or use in tacos.

Marinated Flank Steak

Flo Mast
Broadway, VA

*Gluten-Free option

Makes 4–6 servings

Prep. Time: 10–15 minutes ⚜ *Marinating Time: 3 hours*
Broiling Time: 12 minutes ⚜ *Standing Time: 10 minutes*

½ cup bottled teriyaki sauce
¼ cup soy sauce
4 cloves garlic, chopped
2-lb. flank steak
¼ cup spicy brown mustard

1. In a shallow baking dish, combine the teriyaki sauce, soy sauce, and garlic.

2. Make ¼-inch-deep cuts about ½ inch apart on both sides of the steak, cutting diagonally across the grain.

3. Rub both sides with mustard. Place steak in marinade.

4. Cover and refrigerate for up to 3 hours, turning occasionally.

5. Preheat the broiler and line a shallow pan with foil. Broil for 6 minutes on each side for medium rare, basting once on each side with remaining marinade. Let rest before slicing across grain.

*Recipe Note:

To make this recipe gluten-free, choose a gluten-free teriyaki sauce and swap the soy sauce for tamari soy sauce or liquid aminos.

Oven Enchiladas

Melanie Thrower
McPherson, KS

Gluten-Free option

Makes 8 servings

Prep. Time: 15 minutes ⚬ Cooking/Baking Time: 30 minutes

1 lb. ground beef

2 medium-sized yellow onions, chopped

16 corn tortillas

2 cups shredded Mexican cheese

2 (16-oz.) cans green chili or red enchilada sauce

*Recipe Note:

To make this gluten-free, choose gluten-free enchilada sauce.

1. In a skillet, brown ground beef. Drain off drippings.

2. Heat tortillas in nonstick pan to make them flexible.

3. Fill each tortilla with browned beef, topped with onion. Roll up, tuck in sides, and continue rolling. Place side by side on a baking sheet with sides.

4. Sprinkle cheese over top of filled enchiladas. Pour sauce over top.

5. Cover with aluminum foil. Bake at 375°F for 30 minutes.

Serving suggestion:

Serve with dishes of sour cream, salsa, and guacamole as optional toppings.

Convenient Slow-Cooker Lasagna

Rachel Yoder
Middlebury, IN

*Gluten-Free option, Vegetarian option

Makes 6–8 servings

Prep. Time: 30–45 minutes ❧ Cooking Time: 4 hours ❧ Ideal slow-cooker size: 6-qt.

1 lb. extra-lean ground beef

29-oz. can tomato sauce

8-oz. pkg. lasagna noodles, uncooked, divided

4 cups shredded low-fat mozzarella cheese

1 ½ cups low-fat cottage cheese

*Recipe Notes:

To make this gluten-free, swap the lasagna noodles for gluten-free lasagna noodles, or use thinly-sliced zucchini instead.

To make this recipe vegetarian, swap the ground beef for meatless crumbles.

1. Spray the interior of the cooker with nonstick spray.

2. Brown the ground beef in a large nonstick skillet. Drain off drippings.

3. Stir in tomato sauce. Mix well.

4. Spread one-fourth of the meat sauce on the bottom of the slow cooker.

5. Arrange ⅓ of the uncooked noodles over the sauce. If you wish, break them up so they fit better.

6. Combine the cheeses in a bowl. Spoon ⅓ of the cheeses over the noodles.

7. Repeat these layers twice.

8. Top with remaining meat sauce.

9. Cover and cook on Low 4 hours.

Sloppy Joes

Hope Comerford
Clinton Township, MI

*Gluten-Free

Makes 15–18 servings

Prep. Time: 25 minutes ⚗ Cooking Time: 6–7 hours ⚗ Ideal slow-cooker size: 6-qt.

1 ½ lb. extra-lean ground beef

16 oz. ground turkey sausage

½ large red onion, chopped

½ green bell pepper, chopped

8-oz. can low-sodium tomato sauce

½ cup water

½ cup ketchup

¼ cup tightly packed brown sugar

2 Tbsp. apple cider vinegar

2 Tbsp. yellow mustard

1 Tbsp. gluten-free Worcestershire sauce

1 Tbsp. chili powder

1 tsp. garlic powder

1 tsp. onion powder

¼ tsp. salt

¼ tsp. pepper

1. Brown the ground beef and sausage in a pan. Drain all grease.

2. While the beef and sausage are cooking, mix together the remaining ingredients in the crock.

3. Add the cooked beef and sausage to the crock and mix.

4. Cover and cook on Low for 6–7 hours.

5. Serve on gluten-free hamburger buns (or regular buns if gluten is not a concern).

Stuffed Green Peppers

SLOW-COOKER

Lois Stoltzfus
Honey Brook, PA

Gluten-Free, Vegetarian option, Plant-Based option

Makes 6 servings

Prep. Time: 20 minutes & *Cooking Time: 3–8 hours* & *Ideal slow-cooker size: 5- to 6-qt.*

6 large green peppers
1 lb. extra-lean ground beef, browned
2 Tbsp. minced onion
1 tsp. salt
⅛ tsp. garlic powder
2 cups cooked rice
15-oz. can low-sodium tomato sauce
¾ cup shredded low-fat mozzarella cheese

1. Cut peppers in half and remove seeds.

2. Combine all ingredients except peppers and cheese.

3. Stuff peppers with ground beef mixture. Place in slow cooker.

4. Cover. Cook on Low 6–8 hours, or on High 3–4 hours. Sprinkle with cheese during last 30 minutes.

*Recipe Notes:

To make this recipe vegetarian, swap the ground beef for meatless crumbles.

To make this recipe plant-based, swap the ground beef for meatless crumbles and swap the shredded mozzarella for vegan shredded mozzarella.

Household-Sized Ziti Bake

Joy Reiff
Mount Joy, PA

Gluten-Free option, Vegetarian option

Makes 6–8 servings

Prep. Time: 30 minutes ♣ Baking Time: 45–60 minutes

1 lb. ziti, or rigatoni
1 ¼ lb. ground beef
1 lb. ricotta, or cottage, cheese
½ cup grated Parmesan cheese
3 Tbsp. chopped fresh parsley
1 egg, beaten
½ tsp. salt
¼–½ tsp. pepper, according to your taste preference
6 cups spaghetti sauce
½ lb. mozzarella sauce, shredded

*Recipe Notes:

To make this recipe gluten-free, choose a gluten-free ziti or rigatoni pasta and choose a gluten-free spaghetti sauce.

To make this recipe vegetarian, swap the ground beef for meatless crumbles, or leave it out altogether.

1. Prepare ziti according to package directions. Drain and set aside.

2. Brown ground beef. Stir frequently to break up clumps. Cook until pink no longer remains. Drain off drippings.

3. Stir in ricotta cheese, Parmesan cheese, parsley, egg, salt, and pepper.

4. Add spaghetti sauce. Stir until well mixed.

5. Add ziti. Toss gently to coat well.

6. Spoon into greased 9×13-inch baking pan.

7. Sprinkle with cheese.

8. Bake at 350°F for 45–60 minutes, or until bubbly and heated through.

Pork

Cranberry Glazed Pork Roast

Cova Rexroad
Kingsville, MD

Gluten-Free

Makes 6 servings

Prep. Time: 15 minutes & *Roasting Time: 2 hours* & *Standing Time: 25–30 minutes*

2½–3-lb. pork roast
1 tsp. salt
¼–½ tsp. pepper
16-oz. can whole berry cranberry sauce
½ cup orange juice
¼ cup brown sugar

1. Rub the pork roast with salt and pepper. Bake uncovered at 350°F for 1½ hours.

2. Meanwhile, combine cranberry sauce, orange juice, and brown sugar in a small saucepan. Cook over low heat until mixture comes to a boil, making a thin sauce.

3. After the meat has roasted, brush ¼ of the sauce over the roast and bake uncovered another 30 minutes.

4. Remove the roast from the pan and place it on a serving platter. Cover with foil and allow to stand for 25–30 minutes. Slice thinly and serve with the remaining sauce.

Variation:

For the glaze, use ¼ cup honey, 1 tsp. grated orange peel, ⅛ tsp. cloves, and ⅛ tsp. nutmeg, instead of orange juice and brown sugar.

Savory Pork Roast

Mary Louise Martin
Boyd, WI

*Gluten-Free

Makes 4–6 servings

Prep. Time: 15 minutes   Cooking Time: 3½–4½ hours   Ideal slow-cooker size: 6-qt. oval

4-lb. boneless pork butt roast
I tsp. ground ginger
I Tbsp. fresh minced rosemary
½ tsp. mace or nutmeg
I tsp. coarsely ground black pepper
2 tsp. salt
2 cups water

1. Grease interior of slow-cooker crock.

2. Place roast in the slow cooker.

3. In a bowl, mix spices and seasonings together. Sprinkle half on top of roast, pushing down on spices to encourage them to stick.

4. Flip roast and sprinkle with rest of spices, again, pushing down to make them stick.

5. Pour 2 cups water around the edge, being careful not to wash spices off meat.

6. Cover. Cook on Low 3½–4½ hours, or until instant-read meat thermometer registers 140°F when stuck into center of roast.

Carolina Pot Roast

Jonathan Gehman
Harrisonburg, VA

*Gluten-Free

Makes 3–4 servings

Prep. Time: 20 minutes ♣ Cooking Time: 3 hours ♣ Ideal slow-cooker size: 3-qt.

3 medium-large sweet potatoes, peeled and cut into 1-inch chunks

¼ cup brown sugar

1-lb. pork roast

scant ¼ tsp. cumin

sea salt to taste

water

1. Place sweet potatoes in bottom of slow cooker. Sprinkle brown sugar over potatoes.

2. Heat nonstick skillet over medium-high heat. Add roast and brown on all sides. Sprinkle meat with cumin and salt while browning. Place pork on top of potatoes.

3. Add an inch of water to the cooker, being careful not to wash the seasoning off the meat.

4. Cover and cook on Low 3 hours, or until meat and potatoes are tender but not dry or mushy.

Brown Sugar and Dijon-Marinated Pork Tenderloin

J. B. Miller
Indianapolis, IN

*Gluten-Free option

Makes 4–6 servings

Prep. Time: 5 minutes ⚘ Marinating Time: 2–3 hours ⚘ Grilling Time: 15 minutes

½ cup soy sauce
¼ cup sherry vinegar
½ tsp. Dijon mustard
¼ cup brown sugar
2-lb. pork tenderloin

1. Combine the first four ingredients in a large ziplock plastic bag to make the marinade.

2. Place tenderloin in marinade and close bag. Surround meat with marinade, and then place in refrigerator for 2–3 hours.

3. Heat grill to medium-high. Remove tenderloin from bag, patting dry.

4. Grill tenderloin until desired doneness, 160°F for medium. Thinly slice into medallions and serve.

*Recipe Note:
To make this recipe gluten-free, swap the soy sauce for tamari soy sauce or liquid aminos.

Tips:

1. Be sure grill is hot before placing tenderloin on grill. Tenderloin should have a thin, crisp crust.

2. This is especially good served with garlic mashed potatoes or polenta.

3. You can also prepare the tenderloin in your broiler.

4. Use a meat thermometer to be sure the meat is cooked sufficiently.

Cranberry Pork Tenderloin

SLOW-COOKER

Janice Yoskovich
Carmichaels, PA

*Gluten-Free option

Makes 8 servings

Prep. Time: 10 minutes ⚘ *Cooking Time: 4 hours* ⚘ *Ideal slow-cooker size: 4-qt.*

1½ lb. pork tenderloin
12 oz. chili sauce
16-oz. can jellied cranberry sauce
2 Tbsp. brown sugar
5 cups cooked long-grain enriched rice

1. Place pork tenderloin in slow cooker.

2. Mix together chili sauce, cranberry sauce, and brown sugar. Pour over pork.

3. Cover and cook on Low 4 hours, or until cooked through but not dry.

4. Serve over rice.

*Recipe Note:

To make this recipe gluten-free, choose a gluten-free chili sauce and a gluten-free jellied cranberry sauce.

Salsa Verde Pork

Hope Comerford
Clinton Township, MI

*Gluten-Free

Makes 6 servings

Prep. Time: 20 minutes ❧ *Cooking Time: 6–6½ hours* ❧ *Ideal slow-cooker size: 4-qt.*

1½-lb. boneless pork loin

1 large sweet onion, halved and sliced

2 large tomatoes, chopped

16-oz. jar gluten-free salsa verde (green salsa)

½ cup dry white wine

4 cloves garlic, minced

1 tsp. cumin

½ tsp. chili powder

1. Place the pork loin in the crock and add the rest of the ingredients on top.

2. Cover and cook on Low for 6–6½ hours.

3. Break apart the pork with two forks and mix with contents of crock.

Serving suggestion:

Serve over cooked brown rice or quinoa.

Honey Barbecue Pork Chops

Tamara McCarthy
Pennsburg, PA

*Gluten-Free option

Makes 8 servings

Prep. Time: 15 minutes ⚬ Cooking Time: 6–8 hours ⚬ Ideal slow-cooker size: 4-qt.

8 pork chops, divided
1 large onion, sliced, divided
1 cup barbecue sauce
⅓ cup honey

1. Place one layer of pork chops in your slow cooker.

2. Arrange a proportionate amount of sliced onions over top.

3. Mix barbecue sauce and honey together in a small bowl. Spoon a proportionate amount of sauce over the chops.

4. Repeat the layers.

5. Cover and cook on Low 3–4 hours.

6. If the sauce barely covers the chops, flip them over at this point. If they're well covered, simply allow them to cook another 3–4 hours on Low, or until they're tender but the meat is not dry.

*Recipe Note:

To make this recipe gluten-free, choose a gluten-free barbecue sauce.

Country Ham

Esther Burkholder
Millerstown, PA

*Gluten-Free option

Makes 12 servings

Prep. Time: 10 minutes ❧ *Cooking Time: 6 hours* ❧ *Ideal slow-cooker size: 4-qt.*

3-lb. boneless, fully cooked ham

½–¾ cup brown sugar, according to your taste preferences

2 Tbsp. prepared mustard

¼ cup peach preserves

1. Place ham in slow cooker.

2. Combine remaining ingredients in a small bowl. Spread over ham.

3. Cover and cook on Low for 6 hours, or until heated through.

Variation:

Use apricot preserves instead of peach.
— Edwina Stoltzfus, Narvon, PA

*Recipe Note:

To make this recipe gluten-free, choose gluten-free peach preserves.

Raspberry Balsamic Pork Chops

Hope Comerford
Clinton Township, MI

Gluten-Free

Makes 4–6 servings

Prep. Time: 5 minutes ♣ Cooking Time: 7–8 hours ♣ Ideal slow-cooker size: 3-qt.

SLOW-COOKER

4–5 lb. thick-cut pork chops

¼ cup raspberry balsamic vinegar

2 Tbsp. olive oil

½ tsp. kosher salt

½ tsp. garlic powder

¼ tsp. basil

¼ cup water

1. Place pork chops in the slow cooker.

2. In a small bowl, mix together the remaining ingredients. Pour over the pork chops.

3. Cover and cook on Low for 7–8 hours.

Country Barbecued Ribs

Mary Longenecker
Bethel, PA

*Gluten-Free option

Makes 10 servings

Prep. Time: 10–15 minutes   ⚬   Cooking Time: 8–10 hours   ⚬   Ideal slow-cooker size: 4-qt.

3 lb. lean country-style ribs
2½ lb. sauerkraut, rinsed
2 cups of your favorite barbecue sauce
1 cup water

1. Place ribs on bottom of cooker.

2. Layer sauerkraut over ribs.

3. Mix barbecue sauce and water together. Pour over meat and kraut.

4. Cover. Cook on Low 8–10 hours.

*Recipe Note:

To make this recipe gluten-free, choose a gluten-free barbecue sauce.

Easiest Ever BBQ Country Ribs

SLOW-COOKER

Hope Comerford
Clinton Township, MI

Gluten-Free option

Makes 12 servings

Prep. Time: 5 minutes ⚭ Cooking Time: 8–10 hours ⚭ Ideal slow-cooker size: 6-qt.

4 lb. boneless country ribs

sea salt and pepper to taste

18-oz. bottle of your favorite sugar barbecue sauce

1. Place your country ribs into your crock and sprinkle them with salt and pepper on both sides.

2. Pour half the bottle of barbecue sauce on one side of the ribs. Flip them over and poor the other half of the barbecue sauce on the other side of your ribs. Spread it around.

3. Cover and cook on Low for 8–10 hours.

*Recipe Note:

To make this recipe gluten-free, choose a gluten-free barbecue sauce.

Teriyaki Ribs

Janie Steele
Moore, OK

Makes 2-3 servings

Prep. Time: 10 minutes ❧ Cooking Time: 25 minutes ❧ Setting: Manual
Pressure: High ❧ Release: Natural

½ Tbsp. chopped ginger
1 cup beef broth
½ cup soy sauce
1 Tbsp. minced garlic
4 Tbsp. brown sugar
2 Tbsp. sriracha sauce, or more to taste
⅓ cup hoisin sauce
1 rack ribs (1–2 lb.)

1. Mix all ingredients together in a bowl, except the ribs.

2. Cut ribs into smaller 2–3 rib sections and place in bottom of the inner pot of the Instant Pot.

3. Pour the sauce on top.

4. Secure the lid and make sure vent is at sealing. Set to Manual and cook on high pressure for 25 minutes.

5. Let the pressure release naturally.

6. Serve as is, or if you want crispier coating, set oven to 375°F and bake for about 5 minutes.

7. Reserve sauce from pot as desired for extra moisture.

Carnitas

Hope Comerford
Clinton Township, MI

*Gluten-Free

Makes 12 servings

Prep. Time: 10 minutes 🌿 *Cooking Time: 10–12 hours* 🌿 *Ideal slow-cooker size: 4-qt.*

2-lb. pork shoulder roast
1 ½ tsp. kosher salt
½ tsp. pepper
2 tsp. cumin
5 cloves garlic, minced
1 tsp. oregano
3 bay leaves
2 cups gluten-free, low-sodium chicken stock
2 Tbsp. lime juice
1 tsp. lime zest

1. Place pork shoulder roast in crock.

2. Mix together the salt, pepper, cumin, garlic, and oregano. Rub it onto the pork roast.

3. Place the bay leaves around the pork roast, then pour in the chicken stock around the roast, being careful not to wash off the spices.

4. Cover and cook on Low for 10–12 hours.

5. Remove the roast with a slotted spoon, as well as the bay leaves. Shred the pork between 2 forks, then replace the shredded pork in the crock and stir.

6. Add the lime juice and lime zest to the crock and stir.

7. Serve on warmed white corn tortillas.

Simple Shredded Pork Tacos

Jennifer Freed
Rockingham, AL

*Gluten-Free

Makes 6 servings

Prep. Time: 5 minutes ⚬ Cooking Time: 8 hours ⚬ Ideal slow-cooker size: 4-qt.

2-lb. boneless pork roast
1 cup salsa
4-oz. can chopped green chilies
½ tsp. garlic salt
½ tsp. black pepper

1. Place all ingredients in slow cooker.

2. Cover; cook on Low 8 hours, or until meat is tender.

3. To serve, use 2 forks to shred pork.

Serving suggestion:

Serve with taco shells and your favorite taco fixings.

Italian Subs

OVEN

Susan Kasting
Jenks, OK

*Gluten-Free option

Makes 6 servings

Prep. Time: 15 minutes ⚜ *Cooking/Baking Time: 15 minutes*

6 Italian sausages

1 green bell pepper, sliced in ¼-inch strips

1 red bell pepper, sliced in ¼-inch strips

1 medium-sized onion, sliced in ¼-inch rounds

6 hoagie rolls, split

1. Pan-fry sausages, or grill, until browned on all sides.

2. In a separate pan sprayed with nonstick cooking spray, heat to medium/high heat and sauté the peppers and onions until tender-crisp.

3. Place one sausage and a generous amount of the pepper-onion mix in each hoagie roll. Serve immediately.

*Recipe Note:

To make this recipe gluten-free, choose gluten-free Italian sausages and swap the hoagie rolls for gluten-free sub rolls or bread.

Italian Sausage Dinner

Janessa Hochstedler
East Earl, PA

Makes 6 servings

Prep. Time: 10 minutes & Cooking Time: 5–10 hours & Ideal slow-cooker size: 4-qt.

1 ½ lb. Italian sausage, cut in ¾-inch slices

2 Tbsp. A-1 steak sauce

28-oz. can diced Italian-style tomatoes, with juice

2 chopped green bell peppers

½ tsp. red pepper flakes, optional

2 cups uncooked instant rice

1. Place all ingredients, except rice, in slow cooker.

2. Cover and cook on Low 7½–9½ hours, or on High 4½ hours.

3. Stir in uncooked rice. Cover and cook an additional 20 minutes on High or Low.

Glazed Ham

SLOW-COOKER

Dede Peterson
Rapid City, SD

Gluten-Free option

Makes 4 servings

Prep. Time: 20 minutes ⚖ Cooking Time: 4–6 hours ⚖ Ideal slow-cooker size: 6-qt.

4 ham steaks

⅓ cup apricot jam

¾–1 cup honey, depending upon how much sweetness you like

⅓ cup soy sauce

¼ tsp. nutmeg

1. Place ham in slow cooker.

2. In a bowl, mix all other ingredients together. Pour over ham.

3. Cook on Low 4–6 hours, or until meat is heated through but not dry.

*Recipe Note:

To make this recipe gluten-free, choose gluten-free apricot jam and swap the soy sauce for tamari soy sauce or liquid aminos.

Stromboli

Monica Leaman Kehr
Portland, MI

Makes 6 servings

Prep. Time: 20 minutes & Rising Time: 30–40 minutes
Baking Time: 20 minutes & Standing Time: 10 minutes

1 loaf frozen bread dough, thawed
Italian seasoning
2 cups grated mozzarella cheese
3 oz. sliced pepperoni
4 oz. chipped cooked ham
½ cup sliced black olives
⅓ cup sliced mushrooms, optional
2 Tbsp. chopped onions, optional
2 Tbsp. chopped green or red bell pepper, optional

Tip:

Microwave pepperoni slices between paper towels before putting in stromboli to eliminate some calories.

1. Thaw bread dough and roll to 10×15-inch rectangle on lightly floured surface.

2. Sprinkle dough with Italian seasoning. Cover entire rectangle with cheese, pepperoni, ham, black olives, and any of the other ingredients you want. Press toppings down gently into dough.

3. Starting with the long side of the rectangle, roll dough up into a log shape. Seal ends by pinching dough together.

4. Carefully lift onto a lightly greased baking sheet. Cover and allow to rise 30–40 minutes.

5. Bake on sheet for 20 minutes at 400°F, or until lightly browned.

6. Allow to stand for 10 minutes before slicing.

Chicken and Turkey

Garlic Galore Rotisserie Chicken

INSTANT POT

Hope Comerford
Clinton Township, MI

Gluten-Free

Makes 4 servings

Prep. Time: 5 minutes   ⚮   Cooking Time: 33 minutes   ⚮   Setting: Sauté and Manual
Pressure: High   ⚮   Release: Natural then Manual

3-lb. whole chicken

2 Tbsp. olive oil, divided

salt to taste

pepper to taste

20–30 cloves fresh garlic, peeled and left whole

1 cup chicken stock, broth, or water

2 Tbsp. garlic powder

2 tsp. onion powder

½ tsp. basil

½ tsp. cumin

½ tsp. chili powder

1. Rub chicken with one tablespoon of the olive oil and sprinkle with salt and pepper.

2. Place the garlic cloves inside the chicken. Use butcher's twine to secure the legs.

3. Press the Sauté button on the Instant Pot then add the rest of the olive oil to the inner pot.

4. When the pot is hot, place the chicken inside. You are just trying to sear it, so leave it for about 4 minutes on each side.

5. Remove the chicken and set aside. Place the trivet at the bottom of the inner pot and pour in the chicken stock.

6. Mix together the remaining seasonings and rub it all over the entire chicken.

7. Place the chicken back inside the inner pot, breast side up, on top of the trivet and secure the lid to the sealing position.

8. Press the Manual button and use the +/- to set it for 25 minutes.

9. When the timer beeps, allow the pressure to release naturally for 15 minutes. If the lid will not open at this point, quick release the remaining pressure and remove the chicken.

10. Let the chicken rest for 5–10 minutes before serving.

Traditional Turkey Breast

Hope Comerford
Clinton Township, MI

Gluten-Free

Makes 10–12 servings

Prep. Time: 10 minutes   &   Cooking Time: 8 hours   &   Ideal slow-cooker size: 7-qt.

7-lb. or less turkey breast
2 Tbsp. olive oil

Rub:
2 tsp. garlic powder
1 tsp. onion powder
1 tsp. salt
¼ tsp. pepper
1 tsp. poultry seasoning

1. Remove gizzards from turkey breast, rinse it, and pat dry. Place breast into crock.

2. Rub turkey breast all over with olive oil.

3. Mix together all rub ingredients. Rub this mixture all over turkey breast and press it in.

4. Cover and cook on Low for 8 hours.

Chicken Baked with Red Onions, Potatoes, and Rosemary

Kristine Stalter
Iowa City, IA

Gluten-Free

Makes 8 servings

Prep. Time: 10–15 minutes ⚬ Baking Time: 45–60 minutes

2 red onions, each cut into 10 wedges

1¼ lb. new potatoes, unpeeled and cut into chunks

2 garlic bulbs, separated into cloves, unpeeled

salt and pepper to taste

3 tsp. extra-virgin olive oil

2 Tbsp. balsamic vinegar

approximately 5 sprigs rosemary

8 chicken thighs, skin removed

1. Spread onions, potatoes, and garlic in single layer over bottom of large roasting pan so that they will crisp and brown.

2. Season with salt and pepper.

3. Pour over the oil and balsamic vinegar and add rosemary, leaving some sprigs whole and stripping the leaves off the rest.

4. Toss vegetables and seasonings together.

5. Tuck chicken pieces among vegetables.

6. Bake at 400°F for 45–60 minutes, or until chicken and vegetables are cooked through.

7. Transfer to a big platter, or take to the table in the roasting pan.

Lemon-Chicken Oven Bake

Judi Manos
West Islip, NY

*Gluten-Free option

Makes 4 servings

Prep. Time: 10–15 minutes ⚶ Baking Time: 45–50 minutes

¼ cup zesty Italian dressing
½ cup chicken broth
1 Tbsp. honey
1½ lb. bone-in chicken legs and thighs
1 lb. new potatoes, quartered
5 cloves garlic, peeled
1 lemon, cut in 8 wedges
1 tsp. dried rosemary, optional

*Recipe Note:
To make this recipe gluten-free, choose a gluten-free Italian dressing and choose a gluten-free chicken broth.

1. In a mixing bowl, blend together dressing, broth, and honey.

2. Arrange chicken, potatoes, and garlic in well-greased 9×13-inch baking dish.

3. Drizzle with dressing mixture.

4. Situate lemons and rosemary, if using, among the chicken and potatoes.

5. Bake at 400°F for 45–50 minutes, or until chicken is done and potatoes are tender. (Temperature probe inserted into center of chicken should register 165°F.)

6. Serve lemons as garnish if you wish.

Cranberry Chicken

Judi Manos
West Islip, NY

*Gluten-Free option

Makes 8 servings

Prep. Time: 10 minutes   Baking Time: 50 minutes

4 lb. skinless, bone-in chicken pieces; your choice of breast halves or thighs

16-oz. can whole berry cranberry sauce

8-oz. bottle Catalina dressing

1 envelope onion soup mix

1. Place chicken in single layer in two well-greased 9×13-inch baking dishes.

2. In mixing bowl, blend together cranberry sauce, Catalina dressing, and onion soup mix.

3. Pour over chicken pieces.

4. Bake 50 minutes, or until chicken is done. Thermometer inserted in center of meat should register 165°F.

*Recipe Note:

To make this recipe gluten-free, choose a gluten-free Catalina dressing and choose a gluten-free onion soup mix.

Honey-Glazed Chicken

Laura R. Showalter
Dayton, VA

*Gluten-Free

Makes 6–8 servings

Prep. Time: 10–20 minutes ⚶ Baking Time: 1½ hours

3 lb. chicken pieces
5⅓ Tbsp. (⅓ cup) butter, melted
⅓ cup honey
2 Tbsp. prepared mustard
1 tsp. salt
1 tsp. curry powder, optional

1. Place chicken skin side up in a 9×13-inch baking dish. (The dish is just as tasty if you remove skin from chicken!)

2. Combine remaining ingredients in a small bowl. Pour over chicken.

3. Bake uncovered at 350°F for 1 hour. Baste every 15–20 minutes. Cover and continue baking 30 minutes, or until chicken is tender and juices run clear when pierced with a sharp fork.

Tip:

If you are unable to baste the chicken while baking, double the sauce so that it almost covers the chicken.

Juicy Orange Chicken

Andrea Maher
Dunedin, FL

*Gluten-Free

Makes 6 servings

Prep. Time: 10 minutes ⚬ Cooking Time: 3–8 hours ⚬ Ideal slow-cooker size: 5- or 6-qt.

18–24 oz. boneless, skinless chicken breast, cut into small pieces

1 cup orange juice, no additives

¼ cup honey

6 small oranges, peeled and sliced

¼ cup Bragg's liquid aminos

1. Add all the ingredients to the slow cooker.

2. Cover and cook on High 3–4 hours or Low 6–8 hours.

Serving suggestion:

Serve over broccoli slaw.

Mom's Cornish Hens

Kay Taylor
Florissant, MO

*Gluten-Free

Makes 4 servings

Prep. Time: 25 minutes ⚬ *Cooking/Baking Time: 60 minutes*

half a stick (¼ cup) butter, divided

2 cups carrots, diced

2 cups onion, diced

4 Cornish hens

Lawry's seasoning salt, or equivalent, optional

¼ cup water

1. Melt 2 Tbsp. butter in large skillet.

2. Sauté diced carrots and onions in skillet until crisp tender.

3. Spread vegetables over bottom of 9×13-inch baking pan.

4. Butter hens inside and out with remaining butter. Sprinkle with seasoning salt if you wish.

5. Place hens in pan on top of vegetables.

6. Add ¼ cup water around the hens.

7. Cover. Bake for 30 minutes at 350°F. Uncover. Continue baking for 30 more minutes.

Oven Barbecued Chicken

Carol Eberly
Harrisonburg, VA

*Gluten-Free option

Makes 8–12 servings

Prep. Time: 10 minutes ⚶ Baking Time: 1¼ hours

3 Tbsp. ketchup

2 Tbsp. Worcestershire sauce

2 Tbsp. vinegar

2 Tbsp. soy sauce

3 Tbsp. brown sugar

1 tsp. spicy brown mustard

1 tsp. salt

1 tsp. pepper

8–12 boneless, skinless chicken thighs

1. In a mixing bowl, combine ketchup, Worcestershire sauce, vinegar, soy sauce, brown sugar, mustard, salt, and pepper. Blend well.

2. Lay chicken pieces in one layer in well-greased baking dish.

3. Pour sauce over top.

4. Bake at 350°F for 40 minutes.

5. Turn pieces over. Bake 35 more minutes.

*Recipe Note:

To make this recipe gluten-free, choose a gluten-free Worcestershire sauce and replace the soy sauce with tamari soy sauce or liquid aminos.

Tip:

You can use chicken legs or chicken breasts, too. Check the legs after they've baked for a total of 50 minutes to be sure they're not drying out. Check breasts after they've baked for a total of 30 minutes to be sure they're not becoming dry.

Baked Chicken Fingers

Lori Rohrer
Washington Boro, PA

*Gluten-Free option

Makes 6 servings

Prep. Time: 20 minutes ☙ Baking Time: 20 minutes

1 ½ cups fine, dry bread crumbs

½ cup grated Parmesan cheese

1 ½ tsp. salt

1 Tbsp. dried thyme

1 Tbsp. dried basil

7 boneless, skinless chicken breast halves, cut into 1 ½-inch slices

½ cup butter, melted

*Recipe Note:

To make this recipe gluten-free, replace the bread crumbs with gluten-free bread crumbs.

1. Combine bread crumbs, cheese, salt, and herbs in a shallow bowl. Mix well.

2. Dip chicken pieces in butter, and then into crumb mixture, coating well.

3. Place coated chicken on greased baking sheet in a single layer.

4. Bake at 400°F for 20 minutes.

Variations:

1. In Step 1 use 1 Tbsp. garlic powder, 1 Tbsp. chives, 2 tsp. Italian seasoning, 2 tsp. parsley, ½ tsp. onion salt, ½ tsp. pepper, and ¼ tsp. salt (instead of 1½ tsp. salt, 1 Tbsp. thyme, and 1 Tbsp. basil).
   —Ruth Miller, Wooster, OH

2. Use boneless, skinless chicken thighs, and do not cut them into slices. Bake at 350°F for 20 minutes. Turn chicken. Bake an additional 20 minutes.
   —Eleanor Larson, Glen Lyon, PA

Chicken and Dumplings

Annabelle Unternahrer
Shipshewana, IN

Makes 5–6 servings

Prep. Time: 25 minutes ⚬ Cooking Time: 2½–3½ hours ⚬ Ideal slow-cooker size: 3- or 4-qt.

1 lb. uncooked boneless, skinless chicken breasts, cut in 1-inch cubes

1 lb. frozen vegetables of your choice

1 medium-sized onion, diced

3 cups chicken broth, divided

1½ cups low-fat buttermilk biscuit mix

1. Combine chicken, vegetables, onion, and chicken broth (reserve ½ cup, plus 1 Tbsp., broth) in slow cooker.

2. Cover. Cook on High 2–3 hours.

3. Mix biscuit mix with reserved broth until moistened. Drop by tablespoonfuls over hot chicken and vegetables.

4. Cover. Cook on High 10 minutes.

5. Uncover. Cook on High 20 minutes more.

Simmering Chicken Dinner

Trish Dick
Ladysmith, WI

*Gluten-Free option

Makes 4 servings

Prep. Time: 10 minutes & Cooking Time: 40 minutes

2½ cups chicken broth
½ cup apple juice
1 bay leaf
½ tsp. garlic powder
½ tsp. paprika
¼ tsp. salt
1½ lb. boneless, skinless chicken breasts, or thighs, cut into chunks
1 cup uncooked whole-grain rice
3 cups fresh, or frozen, vegetables (your choice of one, or a mix)
½ tsp. paprika, optional
parsley as garnish, optional

1. Heat chicken broth, apple juice, bay leaf, garlic powder, paprika, and salt in large skillet until boiling, stirring occasionally.

2. Add chicken. Cover. Reduce heat and simmer 10 minutes on low.

3. Turn chicken.

4. Add 1 cup rice around chicken.

5. Top with the vegetables.

6. Cover. Simmer 25 minutes, or until rice is cooked, vegetables are as soft as you like, and chicken is done.

7. Remove bay leaf.

8. Sprinkle with paprika and parsley before serving if you wish.

*Recipe Note:

To make this recipe gluten-free, choose gluten-free chicken broth.

Tip:

If you like a bit of zip, add curry powder in place of paprika.

Salsa Ranch Chicken with Black Beans

Hope Comerford
Clinton Township, MI

*Gluten-Free option

Makes 8 servings

Prep. Time: 10 minutes ⚜ Cooking Time: 5–6 hours ⚜ Ideal slow-cooker size: 3-qt.

2 large boneless, skinless chicken breasts

1 oz. packet low-sodium taco seasoning

1 oz. packet dry ranch dressing mix

1 cup salsa

10½-oz. can condensed cream of chicken soup

15-oz. can black beans, drained, rinsed

sour cream, optional

shredded cheese, optional

*Recipe Note:
To make this recipe gluten-free, choose gluten-free taco seasoning, gluten-free dry ranch dressing mix, and gluten-free cream of chicken soup.

1. Place chicken in crock.

2. In a bowl, mix together the taco seasoning, ranch dressing mix, salsa, cream of chicken soup, and black beans. Pour over the chicken.

3. Cover and cook on Low for 5–6 hours.

4. Serve with sour cream and cheese, if desired.

Serving suggestion:
Serve on top of rice or in a tortilla.

Chicken Parmesan

Jessalyn Wantland
Napoleon, OH

Gluten-Free option

Makes 4 servings

Prep. Time: 10 minutes ⚜ Baking Time: 45 minutes

4 boneless, skinless chicken breast
halves, about 6 oz. each

I egg, beaten

¾ cup Italian-seasoned bread crumbs

25-oz. jar pasta sauce

I cup shredded Parmesan cheese

1. Grease 7×11-inch baking dish.

2. Place egg in shallow bowl.

3. Place bread crumbs in another shallow bowl.

4. Dip each piece of chicken in egg, and then in bread crumbs.

5. Place coated chicken in baking dish.

6. Bake at 400°F for 30 minutes.

7. Spoon pasta sauce over chicken.

8. Top evenly with cheese.

9. Bake another 15 minutes, or until heated through and cheese is melted.

*Recipe Note:

To make this recipe gluten-free, choose gluten-free Italian-seasoned bread crumbs and choose gluten-free pasta sauce.

That's Amore Chicken Cacciatore

Carol Sherwood
Batavia, NY

SLOW-COOKER

*Gluten-Free option

Makes 6 servings

Prep. Time: 20 minutes ⚬ Cooking Time: 7–9 hours ⚬ Ideal slow-cooker size: 6-qt.

6 boneless, skinless chicken breast halves, divided

28-oz. jar spaghetti sauce

2 green peppers, chopped

1 onion, minced

2 Tbsp. minced garlic

*Recipe Note:

To make this recipe gluten-free, choose gluten-free spaghetti sauce.

1. Place a layer of chicken in your slow cooker.

2. Mix remaining ingredients together in a bowl. Spoon half of the sauce over the first layer of chicken.

3. Add remaining breast halves. Top with remaining sauce.

4. Cover and cook on Low 7–9 hours, or until chicken is tender but not dry.

Serving suggestion:

Serve with cooked spaghetti or linguine.

Crispy Ranch Chicken

OVEN

Barb Shirk, Hawkins, WI
Arlene Snyder, Millerstown, PA
Doyle Rounds, Bridgewater, VA
Pat Chase, Fairbank, IA

*Gluten-Free option

Makes 6–8 servings

Prep. Time: 10 minutes ⚘ Baking Time: 20–25 minutes

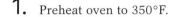

¾–2 cups crispy rice cereal

¾ cup grated Parmesan cheese

1-oz. envelope dry ranch dressing mix

2 egg whites, beaten

8 boneless, skinless chicken thighs, about 5 oz. each

*Recipe Note:

To make this recipe gluten-free, choose a gluten-free crispy rice cereal and a gluten-free dry ranch dressing mix.

1. Preheat oven to 350°F.

2. Spray a large baking sheet with nonstick cooking spray.

3. Combine rice cereal, Parmesan cheese, and dry dressing mix in a large bowl.

4. Place beaten egg whites in a medium-sized bowl.

5. Dip each chicken thigh in the egg whites, and then in the cereal.

6. Arrange the coated chicken on the prepared baking sheet.

7. Bake for about 20–25 minutes, or until chicken is golden and juices run clear when meat is pierced with a knife.

Variations:

1. Substitute crushed cornflakes for the rice cereal.

2. Substitute 1 stick (8 Tbsp.) melted butter for the 2 beaten egg whites.

3. Substitute 8 boneless, skinless chicken breast halves, or 1 cut-up fryer, for the thighs.

Chicken Bruschetta Bake

Krista Hershberger
Elverson, PA

Makes 6 servings

Prep. Time: 15 minutes ❧ *Cooking/Baking Time: 60 minutes*

1½ lb. boneless, skinless chicken breasts, cut into cubes

1 tsp. Italian seasoning

28-oz. can Italian-style stewed tomatoes, well drained

¾ cup shredded mozzarella cheese

6-oz. pkg. stuffing mix for chicken

1½ cups water

1. Preheat oven to 350°F.

2. Place chicken in lightly greased 9×13-inch baking dish. Sprinkle with seasoning.

3. Spread tomatoes over top.

4. Sprinkle with cheese.

5. In a mixing bowl, combine stuffing mix with 1½ cups water. Spoon over baking-pan ingredients.

6. Cover and bake for 30 minutes. Remove cover and bake 30 more minutes.

Easy Chicken Fajitas

Jessica Hontz
Coatesville, PA

*Gluten-Free option

Makes 4–6 servings

Prep. Time: 20 minutes ❦ Marinating Time: 4–8 hours, or overnight ❦ Cooking Time: 10 minutes

1 lb. boneless, skinless chicken breasts
1 pkg. dry Italian salad dressing mix
8-oz. bottle Italian salad dressing
1 cup salsa
1 green pepper, sliced
half a medium-sized onion, sliced
10 (10-inch) flour tortillas

Optional toppings:
shredded Monterey Jack cheese
shredded lettuce
sour cream
chopped tomatoes
salsa
hot pepper sauce

*Recipe Note:
To make this recipe gluten-free, choose gluten-free Italian dressing mix, Italian dressing, and salsa.

1. Cut chicken into thin strips. Place in large mixing bowl.

2. Add dry salad dressing mix and salad dressing. Mix well. Cover and marinade 4–8 hours in the fridge.

3. In a large skillet, combine drained chicken strips, salsa, and pepper and onion slices. Stir-fry until chicken is cooked and peppers and onions are soft.

4. Place chicken mix in tortillas with your choice of toppings.

Variation:

The cooked chicken can also be used on salads.

Easy Chicken Enchiladas

Lois Peterson
Huron, SD

Makes 4 servings

Prep. Time: 35–45 minutes ⚭ *Baking Time: 40 minutes*

10¾-oz. can cream of chicken soup
½ cup sour cream
1 cup picante sauce
2 tsp. chili powder
2 cups chopped cooked chicken
1 cup grated pepper jack cheese
6 (6-inch) flour tortillas
1 medium tomato, chopped
1 green onion, sliced

1. Stir soup, sour cream, picante sauce, and chili powder in a medium bowl.

2. In a large bowl, combine 1 cup sauce mixture, chicken, and cheese.

3. Grease 9×13-inch baking dish.

4. Divide mixture among tortillas.

5. Roll up each tortilla. Place in baking dish, seam side down.

6. Pour remaining sauce mixture over filled tortillas.

7. Cover. Bake at 350°F for 40 minutes or until enchiladas are hot and bubbling.

8. Top with chopped tomato and onion and serve.

Creamy Chicken Rice Casserole

Wanda Roth
Napoleon, OH

*Gluten-Free option

Makes 8 servings

Prep. Time: 20 minutes ⚜ Cooking Time: 2–6 hours ⚜ Ideal slow-cooker size: 6-qt.

1 cup long-grain rice, uncooked
3 cups water
2 tsp. chicken bouillon granules
10¾-oz. can cream of chicken soup
2 cups chopped, cooked chicken breast
¼ tsp. garlic powder
1 tsp. onion salt
1 cup grated cheddar cheese
16-oz. bag frozen broccoli, thawed

1. Combine all ingredients except broccoli in slow cooker.

2. Cook on High a total of 2–3 hours or on Low a total of 4–6 hours.

3. One hour before end of cooking time, stir in broccoli.

*Recipe Note:

To make this recipe gluten-free, choose gluten-free chicken bouillon and a gluten-free cream of chicken soup.

Insta Pasta a la Maria

Maria Shevlin
Sicklerville, NJ

*Gluten-Free option

Makes 6–8 servings

Prep. Time: 10–15 minutes ⚬ Cooking Time: 6 minutes ⚬ Setting: Manual
Pressure: High ⚬ Release: Manual

32-oz. jar of your favorite spaghetti sauce or 1 quart of homemade

2 cups fresh chopped spinach

1 cup chopped mushrooms

½ precooked whole rotisserie chicken, shredded

1 tsp. salt

½ tsp. black pepper

½ tsp. dried basil

¼ tsp. red pepper flakes

1 tsp. parsley flakes

13¼-oz. box pasta, any shape or brand (I used Dreamfield)

3 cups water

*Recipe Note:

To make this recipe gluten-free, choose a gluten-free spaghetti sauce, gluten-free rotisserie chicken, and gluten-free pasta.

1. Place the sauce in the bottom of the inner pot of the Instant Pot.

2. Add in the spinach, then the mushrooms.

3. Add the chicken on top of the veggies and sauce.

4. Add the seasonings and give it a stir to mix.

5. Add the box of pasta.

6. Add 3 cups of water.

7. Secure the lid and move vent to sealing. Set to Manual on high pressure for 6 minutes.

8. When cook time is up, release the pressure manually.

9. Remove the lid and stir to mix together.

Meatless

Vegetable-Stuffed Peppers

Shirley Hinh
Wayland, IA

Gluten-free option, Vegetarian, Plant-Based

Makes 8 servings

Prep. Time: 20 minutes ⚘ Cooking Time: 6–8 hours ⚘ Ideal slow-cooker size: 6-qt.

4 large green, red, or yellow bell peppers
½ cup brown rice
¼ cup minced onions
¼ cup black olives, sliced
2 tsp. liquid aminos
¼ tsp. black pepper
1 clove garlic, minced
28-oz. can whole tomatoes
6-oz. can tomato paste
15¼-oz. can corn or kidney beans, drained

1. Cut tops off peppers (reserve) and remove seeds. Stand peppers up in slow cooker.

2. Mix remaining ingredients in a bowl. Stuff peppers. (You'll have leftover filling.)

3. Place pepper tops back on peppers. Pour remaining filling over the stuffed peppers and work down in between the peppers.

4. Cover and cook on Low 6–8 hours, or until the peppers are done to your liking.

5. If you prefer, you may add ½ cup tomato juice if recipe is too dry.

6. Cut peppers in half and serve.

Serving suggestion:
Drizzle with Greek yogurt if you are not vegan.

Vegetarian Black Bean Burritos

Maricarol Magill
Freehold, NJ

OVEN

*Vegetarian, Plant-Based option

Makes 8 burritos

Prep. Time: 10 minutes ⚭ *Cooking/Baking Time: 40 minutes*

1¼ cups water
1 Tbsp. butter
½ cup long-grain rice
½ tsp. salt
8 (10-inch) flour tortillas
10-oz. pkg. frozen corn
15-oz. can spicy black-bean chili
8-oz. can tomato sauce
shredded cheddar, Monterey Jack, or pepper jack cheese

*Recipe Note:

To make this recipe plant-based, replace the butter with vegan butter and choose vegan shredded cheeses.

1. In a medium-sized saucepan, bring water and butter to a boil.

2. Stir in rice and salt. Cover. Simmer over low heat until rice is cooked, about 20 minutes.

3. Meanwhile, wrap tortillas in foil. Heat oven to 350°F and then heat tortillas until warm, about 15 minutes.

4. When rice is done, stir in corn, black bean chili, and tomato sauce. Heat to boiling over medium-high heat. Boil one minute.

5. Assemble burritos by spooning rice mixture onto tortillas. Top with cheese of your choice. Fold in tops of tortillas and roll up.

Chile Rellenos Casserole

Elena Yoder
Albuquerque, NM

Gluten-Free option, Vegetarian

Makes 12 servings

Prep. Time: 30 minutes ⚘ *Baking Time: 35–40 minutes*

I can of 18–20 whole green chilies
I lb. Monterey Jack cheese
sprinkle of garlic salt
4 eggs
I Tbsp. flour
I cup milk
¾ tsp. salt
¼–½ tsp. pepper
½ lb. cheddar, or longhorn, cheese, grated

*Recipe Note:

To make this recipe gluten-free, replace the flour with a gluten-free flour blend.

1. Spray 9×13-inch baking pan with nonstick cooking spray.

2. Wearing gloves, cut chilies in half and remove seeds and membranes.

3. Cut Monterey Jack cheese into strips. Place strips in chili halves. Place stuffed chilies in pan side by side, cut side up.

4. Sprinkle with garlic salt.

5. In a mixing bowl, beat eggs. Stir in flour, milk, salt, and pepper.

6. Pour over chilies.

7. Sprinkle with grated cheese.

8. Bake at 350°F for 35–40 minutes, or until set and beginning to brown.

Tip:

You can put this together the day before you want to serve it. Or stuff the chilies and freeze them until you need a quick meal. Then proceed with Step 5.

Mjadra

Hope Comerford
Clinton Township, MI

*Gluten-Free, Vegetarian, Plant-Based

Makes 4–6 servings

Prep. Time: 1 hour 20 minutes ⚜ *Cooking Time: 20–25 minutes*

½ cup olive oil

2 large sweet onions, chopped

1 cup dried lentils

4 cups water

¼ cup lemon juice

⅛ tsp. pepper

1 tsp. salt

1 cup uncooked white rice

1. Heat the olive oil over medium-high heat. Add the onions and let brown lightly. Reduce the heat to low and cover. Let the onions caramelize for at least 1 hour.

2. Rinse the lentils then add them to the water. Bring to a boil and cook for 15 minutes.

3. When the onions are done, mix them with the cooked lentils, lemon juice, pepper, salt, and uncooked white rice.

4. Cover and cook for 20–25 minutes, or until the rice and lentils are fluffy.

Serving suggestion:

Serve with pita bread (vegetarian or plant-based) or on a bed of lettuce (gluten-free, vegetarian, plant-based).

Vegetarian Lasagna Roll-Ups

OVEN

Judy Buller
Bluffton, OH

Gluten-Free option, Vegetarian

Makes 12 servings

Prep. Time: 30 minutes ❧ Baking Time: 25–30 minutes

12 uncooked lasagna noodles

2 eggs, slightly beaten

2½ cups ricotta cheese

2½ cups (10 oz.) shredded mozzarella cheese, divided

½ cup Parmesan cheese

1 pkg. frozen, chopped spinach, thawed and squeezed dry, or 4 cups chopped fresh spinach that has been microwaved on High 1–2 minutes and squeezed dry

¼ tsp. salt

¼ tsp. pepper

1–2 cups black beans, rinsed

23½-oz. jar spaghetti sauce, your favorite variety, divided

*Recipe Note:

To make this recipe gluten-free, choose gluten-free lasagna noodles and a gluten-free spaghetti sauce.

1. Cook lasagna noodles according to box directions. Drain and rinse well. Lay flat.

2. In a good-sized mixing bowl, mix together eggs, ricotta cheese, 1½ cups mozzarella cheese, Parmesan cheese, spinach, salt, and pepper.

3. Spread about ⅓ cup mixture on each noodle.

4. Sprinkle each noodle with black beans. Press down to make beans adhere.

5. Spread 1 cup spaghetti sauce in bottom of well-greased 9×13-inch baking pan.

6. Roll up noodles and place seam-side down in baking pan.

7. Top rolls with remaining sauce. Sprinkle with 1 cup mozzarella cheese.

8. Bake uncovered at 350°F for 25–30 minutes, or until heated through.

Tip:

You can assemble this dish ahead of time through Step 7, and then freeze or refrigerate it until you're ready to use it. Allow more time to bake if the dish is cold, probably 45–50 minutes total. But check while baking so as not to have it dry out or be overbaked.

Tortellini with Broccoli

Susan Kasting
Jenks, OK

Vegetarian

Makes 4 servings

Prep. Time: 10 minutes ❧ Cooking Time: 2½–3 hours ❧ Ideal slow-cooker size: 4-qt.

½ cup water

26-oz. jar your favorite pasta sauce, divided

1 Tbsp. Italian seasoning

9-oz. pkg. frozen spinach and cheese tortellini

16-oz. pkg. frozen broccoli florets

1. In a bowl, mix water, pasta sauce, and seasoning together.

2. Pour ⅓ of sauce into bottom of slow cooker. Top with all the tortellini.

3. Pour ⅓ of sauce over tortellini. Top with broccoli.

4. Pour remaining sauce over broccoli.

5. Cook on High 2½–3 hours, or until broccoli and pasta are tender but not mushy.

Super Creamy Macaroni and Cheese

Jean Butzer, Batavia, NY
Arlene Leaman Kliewer, Lakewood, CO
Esther Burkholder, Millerstown, PA
Hazel Lightcap Propst, Oxford, PA
Karla Baer, North Lima, OH

*Vegetarian option

Makes 8–10 servings

Prep. Time: 5–10 minutes ❧ Baking Time: 1 hour 20 minutes

1 lb. uncooked elbow macaroni

4 cups shredded cheddar cheese, or ½ lb. cubed Velveeta cheese

2 (10¾-oz.) cans cheddar cheese, or cream of celery, soup

3½ cups milk

1½ cups cooked ham, chopped, optional

1 tsp. salt, optional

¼ tsp. pepper, optional

1. Combine all ingredients in a buttered 3-qt. casserole or baking dish.

2. Cover and bake at 350°F for 1 hour.

3. Stir up from bottom.

4. Bake uncovered an additional 20 minutes.

*Recipe Note:

To make this vegetarian, leave out the optional ham.

Shrimp with Sun-Dried Tomatoes

Josie Healy
Middle Village, NY

*Gluten-Free

Makes 3–4 servings

Prep. Time: 10 minutes & Cooking Time: 10 minutes

2 Tbsp. olive oil

I lb. cleaned and peeled shrimp

2 cloves garlic, minced

¼ cup white wine

6–8 sun-dried tomatoes, chopped (use dry tomatoes, not in oil)

1. Place olive oil in large skillet and heat. Carefully add shrimp and garlic, being careful not to splatter yourself with the hot oil.

2. Sauté, stirring constantly, until shrimp is slightly pink and garlic is softened.

3. Stir in wine and sun-dried tomatoes. Cook another 1–2 minutes over low heat.

4. If you'd like more liquid, add ¼ cup water, more wine, or chicken stock.

5. Serve over rice or pasta.

Sides

Brown Sugar Glazed Carrots

Michele Ruvola
Vestal, NY

*Gluten-Free option, Vegetarian, Plant-Based option

Makes 10 servings

Prep. Time: 5 minutes   ⚬   Cooking Time: 4 minutes   ⚬   Setting: Steam
Pressure: High   ⚬   Release: Manual

32-oz. bag of baby carrots
½ cup vegetable broth
½ cup brown sugar
4 Tbsp. butter
½ Tbsp. salt

1. Place all ingredients in inner pot of the Instant Pot.

2. Secure the lid, turn valve to sealing, and set timer for 4 minutes on Manual at high pressure.

3. When cooking time is up, perform a quick release to release pressure.

4. Stir carrots, then serve.

*Recipe Notes:

To make this recipe gluten-free, use gluten-free vegetable broth.

To make this recipe plant-based, replace the butter with vegan butter or coconut oil.

Roasted Baby Carrots

OVEN

Melanie Mohler
Ephrata, PA

*Gluten-Free, Vegetarian, Plant-Based

Makes 4–5 servings

Prep. Time: 5–10 minutes 🍴 Cooking/Roasting Time: 10–15 minutes

I lb. baby carrots
I Tbsp. olive oil
I Tbsp. dried dill weed
sprinkle of salt

1. Preheat oven to 475°F.

2. If using thick baby carrots, slice in half lengthwise. Otherwise leave as is.

3. In a large bowl, combine olive oil and dill. Add carrots and toss to coat.

4. In a 10×15-inch baking pan, spread carrots in a single layer.

5. Roast, uncovered, about 10 minutes or until carrots are just tender, stirring once.

6. Sprinkle with salt before serving.

Roasted Broccoli

Andrea Cunningham
Arlington, KS

*Gluten-Free, Vegetarian, Plant-Based

Makes 4 servings

Prep. Time: 10 minutes   Baking Time: 20 minutes

I head (about 5 cups) broccoli, cut into long pieces all the way through (you will eat the stems)

I Tbsp. olive oil

2–3 cloves garlic, sliced thin

sprinkle of pepper

lemon wedges

1. Preheat oven to 400°F.

2. Place broccoli in baking pan with sides. Drizzle with olive oil. Toss to coat.

3. Sprinkle garlic and pepper over top.

4. Transfer to oven and roast 15–20 minutes, or until broccoli is crispy on the ends and a little browned.

5. Sprinkle with lemon juice.

Cheesy Broccoli

OVEN

Esther J. Mast
Lancaster, PA

Jan Rankin
Millersville, PA

*Vegetarian

Makes 6–8 servings

Prep. Time: 20 minutes   Baking Time: 20 minutes

2 (10-oz.) pkgs. frozen broccoli
1 stick (8 Tbsp.) butter, melted, divided
8-oz. pkg. Velveeta cheese, grated, divided
36–38 Ritz crackers (about ⅔ tube), crushed

1. Place broccoli in a medium-sized saucepan, along with about ¼ cup water. Cover and steam, stirring occasionally, until crisp-tender, about 5–10 minutes.

2. Drain broccoli and place in lightly greased 1½-qt. casserole.

3. Pour half of melted butter over broccoli.

4. Stir in most of the cheese. Reserve the rest for sprinkling on top of fully mixed casserole.

5. In a mixing bowl, combine the remaining butter with the crushed crackers. Sprinkle over broccoli mixture.

6. Top with reserved cheese.

7. Bake uncovered at 325°F for 20 minutes.

Cheesy Cauliflower

Joan Erwin
Sparks, NV

Gluten-Free, Vegetarian

Makes 4–5 servings

Prep. Time: 5–10 minutes ⚹ Cooking Time: 10 minutes

I head cauliflower

I Tbsp. water

I cup mayonnaise

I Tbsp. prepared mustard

½ cup chopped green or red onions

I cup shredded Monterey Jack and cheddar cheeses, combined, or one of the two

1. Place whole cauliflower head in microwavable glass baking dish. Add water. Cover. Microwave on High for 9 minutes, until crisp-cooked.

2. Meanwhile, combine mayonnaise, mustard, and onions in a small bowl. Spread over cooked cauliflower. Sprinkle with cheese.

3. Cover and microwave on High for 1 minute, or until cheese is melted.

Variation:

You may break the cauliflower into florets and proceed with Step 1.

Maple-Glazed Squash

OVEN

Jean Turner
Williams Lake, BC

*Gluten-Free option, Vegetarian, Plant-Based option

Makes 6–8 servings

Prep. Time: 10–15 minutes ✧ Baking Time: 50–55 minutes

2 acorn squash
salt and pepper
⅔ cup maple syrup
½ cup soft bread crumbs
½ stick (4 Tbsp.) butter, softened

1. Trim off ends of acorn squash, then cut crosswise into 1-inch slices. Discard seeds.

2. Season squash with salt and pepper.

3. Arrange a single layer of squash in a large shallow baking pan. Cover and bake at 350°F for 30–35 minutes.

4. Combine syrup, crumbs, and butter in a small mixing bowl. Spread over squash.

5. Bake uncovered for 15–20 minutes, basting occasionally.

*Recipe Notes:

To make this recipe gluten-free, use gluten-free bread crumbs.

To make this recipe plant-based, use vegan butter instead of regular butter.

Oven Brussels Sprouts

Gail Martin
Elkhart, IN

*Gluten-Free, Vegetarian, Plant-Based

Makes 8 servings

Prep. Time: 15 minutes ⚬ Baking Time: 15–20 minutes

1 ½ lb. Brussels sprouts, halved
¼ cup plus 2 Tbsp. olive oil
juice of 1 lemon
½ tsp. salt
½ tsp. pepper
½ tsp. crushed red pepper flakes

1. In a large bowl, toss halved sprouts with 2 Tbsp. olive oil.

2. Place them on a single layer on a rimmed cookie sheet.

3. Roast sprouts in the oven at 450°F, stirring twice, until crisp and lightly browned, about 15–20 minutes.

4. Whisk together in a large bowl ¼ cup oil, lemon juice, salt, pepper, and crushed red pepper.

5. Toss sprouts with dressing and serve.

 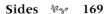

Zucchini Ribbons

Delores Gnagey
Saginaw, MI

*Gluten-Free, Vegetarian, Plant-Based

Makes 4 servings

Prep. Time: 15 minutes & *Cooking Time: 9 minutes*

I large zucchini, unpeeled, ends trimmed

I Tbsp. olive oil

3 cloves garlic, minced

I cup cherry tomato halves

½ tsp. dried basil

pepper to taste

1. With vegetable peeler, slice zucchini into long, lengthwise strips, thick enough not to bend. (If strips are too thin, they'll get mushy while sautéing.)

2. Heat oil in large skillet over medium heat. Add zucchini ribbons. Sauté 4 minutes.

3. Add garlic and sauté 2 more minutes.

4. Add cherry tomatoes and sauté 2 additional minutes.

5. Sprinkle with basil and pepper to taste. Cook 1 minute.

Baked Corn

Phyllis Good
Lancaster, PA

Gluten-Free, Vegetarian

Makes 6 servings

Prep. Time: 20 minutes ⚬ *Baking Time: 30–45 minutes*

3 eggs

2 cups fresh or frozen corn, creamed or simply cut off the cob

2 cups milk

1 Tbsp. butter, melted

salt and pepper to taste

1. In a large mixing bowl, beat eggs well.

2. Stir in the remaining ingredients.

3. Pour into a lightly greased 1½- or 2-qt. greased casserole.

4. Bake uncovered at 325°F for 30–45 minutes, or until knife inserted in center comes out clean.

Chili-Lime Corn on the Cob

Hope Comerford
Clinton Township, MI

Gluten-Free, Vegetarian, Plant-Based option

Makes 6 servings

Prep. Time: 10 minutes & Cooking Time: 4 hours & Ideal slow-cooker size: 6-qt.

6 ears corn, shucked and cleaned

3 tsp. butter, at room temperature

2 Tbsp. freshly squeezed lime juice

1 tsp. lime zest

2 tsp. chili powder

1 tsp. salt

½ tsp. pepper

1. Tear off 6 pieces of aluminum foil to fit each ear of corn. Place each ear of corn on a piece of foil.

2. Mix together butter, lime juice, lime zest, chili powder, salt, and pepper.

3. Divide butter mixture evenly among six ears of corn and spread it over ears of corn. Wrap them tightly with foil so they don't leak.

4. Place the foil-wrapped ears of corn into crock. Cover and cook on Low for 4 hours.

*Recipe Note:

To make this recipe plant-based, replace butter with vegan butter or use coconut oil.

Roasted Asparagus

Barbara Walker
Sturgis, SD

*Gluten-Free, Vegetarian, Plant-Based

Makes 6 servings

Prep. Time: 5 minutes   *Cooking Time: 12 minutes*

1 lb. fresh asparagus spears
2–3 Tbsp. olive oil
⅛ tsp. pepper
2 Tbsp. balsamic vinegar

1. Place asparagus in bowl with olive oil. Toss together to coat asparagus.

2. Place asparagus spears on a baking sheet in a single layer. Sprinkle with pepper.

3. Roast uncovered at 450°F. Shake pan once or twice to turn spears after about 6 minutes.

4. Roast another 6 minutes, or until asparagus is tender-crisp.

5. Put on a plate and drizzle with balsamic vinegar. Serve immediately.

Lemony Garlic Asparagus

SLOW-COOKER

Hope Comerford
Clinton Township, MI

Gluten-Free, Vegetarian, Plant-Based

Makes 4 servings

Prep. Time: 5 minutes ⚬ *Cooking Time: 1½–2 hours* ⚬ *Ideal slow-cooker size: 2- or 3-qt.*

1 lb. asparagus, bottom inch (tough part) removed

1 Tbsp. olive oil

1½ Tbsp. lemon juice

3–4 cloves garlic, peeled and minced

¼ tsp. salt

⅛ tsp. pepper

1. Spray crock with nonstick spray.

2. Lay asparagus at bottom of crock and coat with the olive oil.

3. Pour the lemon juice over the top, then sprinkle with the garlic, salt, and pepper.

4. Cover and cook on Low for 1½–2 hours.

Fresh Green Beans

SLOW-COOKER

Lizzie Ann Yoder
Hartville, OH

*Gluten-Free option, Vegetarian option, Plant-Based option

Makes 6–8 servings

Prep. Time: 20 minutes & Cooking Time: 6–24 hours & Ideal slow-cooker size: 4- to 5-qt.

¼ lb. turkey bacon pieces

2 lb. fresh green beans, washed and cut into pieces or frenched

3–4 cups water

1 scant tsp. sea salt

1. Cut bacon into squares and brown in nonstick skillet. When crispy, drain and set aside.

2. Place all ingredients in slow cooker. Mix together well.

3. Cover and cook on High 6–10 hours or on Low 10–24 hours, or until beans are done to your liking.

*Recipe Notes:

To make this recipe gluten-free, choose a gluten-free turkey bacon, or use regular gluten-free bacon.

To make this recipe vegetarian and/or plant-based, use a meatless "bacon" instead of turkey bacon.

Holiday Green Beans

Joanne Kennedy
Plattsburgh, NY
Jean Ryan
Peru, NY

Gluten-Free, Vegetarian, Plant-Based

Makes 10 servings

Prep. Time: 10 minutes ⚜ *Cooking Time: 20 minutes*

2 lb. (about 8 cups) fresh green beans
1 large red onion, thinly sliced
3 cloves fresh garlic, minced
1 tsp. olive oil
½ cup slivered almonds
pepper to taste

1. Steam beans in saucepan until just slightly crisp.

2. Sauté onion and garlic in olive oil in large skillet for 3 minutes.

3. Add beans to skillet. Sauté 1 minute.

4. Add slivered almonds and pepper to beans. Toss together and then serve.

Sugar Snap Pea Crunchies

Joy Uhler
Richardson, TX

*Gluten-Free, Vegetarian, Plant-Based

Makes 4–12 servings (salad/side or snack/appetizer)

Prep. Time: 6–8 minutes

½ lb. fresh sugar snap peas, washed
1 Tbsp. sesame oil
2 tsp. toasted sesame seeds
¼ tsp. salt, optional

1. Pinch off ends and any strings from each pea pod.

2. Place in mixing bowl.

3. Toss raw peas with sesame oil.

4. Sprinkle toasted sesame seeds, and salt if using, over all and toss together.

5. Serve as a vegetable side dish, a salad, or as finger food for a snack or appetizer.

Tips:

1. Store these peas in an airtight container. Just take the lid off and eat or serve. Refrigerate if you won't be eating the peas immediately. Serve chilled or at room temperature.

2. You can find the oil and seeds in the Asian food section of your grocery store.

Healthy Sweet Potato Fries

Gladys M. High
Ephrata, PA

Gluten-Free, Vegetarian, Plant-Based

Makes 4 servings

Prep. Time: 15 minutes ⚹ Roasting Time: 30 minutes

organic olive oil cooking spray

2 large sweet potatoes, peeled and cut into wedges

¼ tsp. salt

¼ tsp. black pepper

oregano, thyme, rosemary, garlic powder, optional

1. Preheat oven to 400°F.

2. Coat baking sheet with organic olive oil cooking spray.

3. Arrange potato wedges on baking sheet in a single layer. Coat with cooking spray.

4. Sprinkle potatoes with salt, pepper, and any additional seasonings of your choice.

5. Roast 30 minutes, or until tender and golden brown.

Maple-Glazed Sweet Potatoes

Jan Mast
Lancaster, PA

*Gluten-Free option, Vegetarian, Plant-Based option

Makes 8–10 servings

Prep. Time: 20 minutes ❧ *Cooking Time: 3–4 hours* ❧ *Ideal slow-cooker size: 2-qt.*

8–10 medium-sized sweet potatoes
½ tsp. salt
½ cup maple syrup
1 Tbsp. butter
1 Tbsp. flour
¼ cup water

1. Cook sweet potatoes in 2–3 inches water in a large saucepan until barely soft. Drain. When cool enough to handle, peel and slice into slow cooker.

2. While potatoes are cooking in the saucepan, combine remaining ingredients in a microwave-safe bowl.

3. Microwave on High for 1½ minutes. Stir. Repeat until glaze thickens slightly.

4. Pour glaze over peeled, cooked sweet potatoes in slow cooker.

5. Cover and cook on High 3–4 hours.

*Recipe Notes:

To make this recipe gluten-free, replace the flour with a gluten-free flour blend.

To make this recipe plant-based, replace the butter with vegan butter or coconut oil.

Bacon Ranch Red Potatoes

Hope Comerford
Clinton Township, MI

*Gluten-Free option, Vegetarian option, Plant-Based option

Makes 6 servings

Prep. Time: 15 minutes ⚶ Cooking Time: 7 minutes ⚶ Setting: Sauté then Manual
Pressure: High ⚶ Release: Manual

4 strips bacon, chopped into small pieces

2 lb. red potatoes, diced

1 Tbsp. fresh chopped parsley

1 tsp. sea salt

4 cloves garlic, chopped

1-oz. packet ranch dressing/seasoning mix

⅓ cup water

½ cup shredded sharp white cheddar

2 Tbsp. chopped green onions for garnish

1. Set the Instant Pot to Sauté, add the bacon to the inner pot, and cook until crisp.

2. Stir in the potatoes, parsley, sea salt, garlic, ranch dressing seasoning, and water.

3. Secure the lid, make sure vent is at sealing, then set the Instant Pot to Manual for 7 minutes at high pressure.

4. When cooking time is up, do a quick release and carefully open the lid.

5. Stir in the cheese. Garnish with the green onions.

*Recipe Notes:

To make this recipe gluten-free, choose a gluten-free packet of ranch dressing mix.

To make this recipe vegetarian, skip the bacon and skip Step 1. Add 1 Tbsp. olive oil.

To make this recipe plant-based, skip the bacon and skip Step 1. Add 1 Tbsp. olive oil. Replace the white cheddar with vegan shredded cheddar.

Ranch Potato Cubes

OVEN

Charlotte Shaffer
East Earl, PA

*Gluten-Free option, Vegetarian

Makes 8 servings

Prep. Time: 20 minutes ⚹ *Baking Time: 1 hour 10 minutes*

6 medium potatoes, cut into ½-inch cubes
½ stick (4 Tbsp.) butter, cubed
1 cup sour cream
1 packet ranch salad dressing mix
1 cup (4 oz.) shredded cheddar cheese

1. Place potatoes in a greased 7×11-inch baking dish. Dot with butter.

2. Cover. Bake at 350°F for 1 hour.

3. Combine sour cream and salad dressing mix.

4. Spoon over potatoes. Sprinkle with cheese.

5. Bake uncovered 10 minutes until cheese is melted.

*Recipe Note:

To make this recipe gluten-free, choose a gluten-free ranch dressing mix.

Rosemary Roasted Potatoes

Pamela Pierce
Annville, PA

Gluten-Free, Vegetarian, Plant-Based

Makes 8 servings

Prep. Time: 10 minutes   ⚘   Baking Time: 45–60 minutes

8 medium red potatoes, scrubbed, dried, and cut into wedges

3 Tbsp. olive oil

1 tsp. crushed dried rosemary

1 tsp. crushed dried thyme

½ tsp. salt

⅛ tsp. pepper

1. Toss potato wedges in oil.

2. Place in shallow roasting pan and sprinkle evenly with seasonings. Stir.

3. Roast in 375°F oven for 45–60 minutes, stirring every 10–15 minutes, until golden and fork-tender.

Scalloped Potatoes

Hope Comerford
Clinton Township, MI

*Gluten-Free option, Vegetarian option

Makes 10–12 servings

Prep. Time: 25 minutes ❧ Cooking Time: 5 hours
Standing Time: 15–20 minutes ❧ Ideal slow-cooker size: 6- or 7-qt.

I cup nonfat plain Greek yogurt

I cup reduced-sodium chicken stock
or vegetable stock

I Tbsp. salted butter, melted

4 Tbsp. flour

3 cloves garlic, minced

I Tbsp. chopped fresh thyme

½ tsp. dry ground mustard

I tsp. sea salt

¼ tsp. pepper

10 cups peeled and sliced (about ⅛-
inch thick) russet potatoes

½ cup chopped onion

8 oz. low-fat extra-sharp shredded
cheddar cheese

1. Spray crock well with nonstick cooking spray.

2. In a bowl, mix together the yogurt, chicken stock, butter, flour, garlic, dry ground mustard, sea salt, and pepper.

3. Arrange ⅓ of the potatoes on the bottom of the crock, overlapping each slightly. Sprinkle them with ⅓ of the chopped onions, ⅓ of the cheese, then pour ⅓ of the sauce you mixed in the bowl over the top. Repeat this process two more times.

4. Make sure the potatoes are submerged. Press them down if needed. Cover and cook on Low for 5 hours. Let stand for 15–20 minutes, or until thickened.

*Recipe Notes:

To make this recipe gluten-free, choose a gluten-free chicken or vegetable stock.

To make this recipe vegetarian, choose the vegetable stock option.

Country-Style Baked Beans

Rhoda Atzeff
Lancaster, PA

*Gluten-Free

Makes 8 servings

Prep. Time: 10–15 minutes ⚘ *Cooking Time: 12–15 minutes* ⚘ *Standing Time: 5 minutes*

2 (16-oz.) cans pinto beans, drained

I cup chopped ham

½ cup Bull's-Eye Original barbecue sauce

½ cup finely chopped onion

2 Tbsp.–¼ cup molasses, depending on your taste preference

1. Combine ingredients in a lightly greased 1½-qt. casserole. Cover with waxed paper.

2. Microwave on High 12–15 minutes, or until thoroughly heated, stirring every 5 minutes.

3. Let stand 5 minutes before serving.

Lightly Sweet Cornbread

Hope Comerford
Clinton Township, MI

Gluten-Free option, Vegetarian

Makes 6 servings

Prep. Time: 10 minutes 🍃 Cooking Time: 3½–4 hours 🍃 Ideal slow-cooker size: 3-qt.

1 cup cornmeal
1 cup flour
⅓ cup sugar
2 tsp. baking powder
2 Tbsp. butter, melted
¼ cup canola oil
1 egg
1–2 Tbsp. honey
1 cup nonfat milk
¼ cup frozen corn, optional

1. In a bowl, mix the cornmeal, flour, sugar, and baking powder.

2. Next, add the melted butter, oil, egg, honey, and milk and mix it up.

3. Add the corn (if using) and stir again.

4. Grease your crock with nonstick spray and pour in the batter.

5. Cover and cook on Low for 3½–4 hours.

*Recipe Note:

To make this recipe gluten-free, replace the flour with a gluten-free flour blend.

Spaghetti Salad

Lois Stoltzfus
Honey Brook, PA

Gluten-Free option, Vegetarian option, Plant-Based option

Makes 6–8 servings

Prep. Time: 15 minutes ⚬ Cooking Time: 15 minutes ⚬ Cooling Time: 30 minutes

16-oz. box angel-hair pasta
½ cup vegetable, or olive, oil
½ cup lemon juice
1 Tbsp. seasoned salt
½ cup mayonnaise
1 green bell pepper, chopped
1 cup grape tomatoes
1 red onion, chopped
1 cup grated cheddar cheese
½ cup black olives, sliced
pepperoni, optional

1. Cook pasta according to directions.

2. Mix oil, lemon juice, seasoned salt, and mayonnaise together. Add to drained pasta while it is still warm.

3. When pasta mixture has cooled at least 30 minutes, stir in pepper, tomatoes, onion, cheese, olives, and optional pepperoni. Chill.

*Recipe Notes:

To make this recipe gluten-free, change out the angel-hair pasta for gluten free spaghetti, and choose a gluten-free seasoned salt.

To make this vegetarian, leave out the optional pepperoni.

To make this recipe plant-based, replace the mayonnaise with vegan mayo and the cheddar cheese with vegan cheese. Leave out the optional pepperoni.

Picnic Pea Salad

Mary Kathryn Yoder
Harrisonville, MO

Gluten-Free option, Vegetarian option

Makes 4–6 servings

Prep. Time: 30 minutes   ⚓   Chilling Time: 1 hour

10-oz. pkg. frozen peas, thawed
¼ cup chopped onion, or green onions
½ cup chopped celery
½ cup sour cream
2 Tbsp. mayonnaise
1 tsp. salt
1 tsp. dill weed
¼ tsp. pepper
1 cup Spanish peanuts
¼–½ cup fried and crumbled bacon
1 cup cherry tomatoes for garnish, optional

1. Mix peas, onion, celery, sour cream, mayonnaise, salt, dill weed, and pepper. Chill.

2. Just before serving, stir in peanuts. Garnish with bacon and tomatoes.

Variation:

Omit celery, peanuts, and dill weed. Add a chopped hard-boiled egg and a dash of garlic powder.

—Dorothy VanDeest, Memphis, TN

*Recipe Notes:

To make this recipe gluten-free, choose gluten-free bacon.

To make this recipe vegetarian, use meatless bacon instead of regular bacon or leave out the bacon.

Simple Broccoli Slaw

Hope Comerford
Clinton Township, MI

Gluten-Free, Vegetarian, Plant-Based

Makes 4 cups

Prep. Time: 5 minutes • Chilling Time: 30 minutes

4 cups broccoli slaw

Dressing:

¼ cup olive oil

¼ cup apple cider vinegar

2 Tbsp. sugar

½ tsp. mustard powder

½ tsp. garlic powder

½ tsp. onion powder

1. Place slaw in bowl. Mix together all of the dressing ingredients. Pour this over the broccoli slaw.

2. Refrigerate for 30 minutes or longer.

*Recipe Notes:

Add shredded carrot to the broccoli slaw if desired.

Spinach Salad Caprese

Jan Moore
Wellsville, KS

Gluten-Free, Vegetarian

Makes 4 servings

Prep. Time: 10–20 minutes

6 cups fresh spinach
12 cherry tomatoes, halved
½ cup chopped fresh basil
4 oz. fresh mozzarella cheese, cubed
¼ cup light olive oil

1. Gently combine all ingredients.

2. Toss to mix.

3. Serve immediately.

Simple Gluten-Free Tabbouleh

QUICK & EASY

Hope Comerford
Clinton Township, MI

Gluten-Free, Vegetarian, Plant-Based

Makes about 8 servings

Prep. Time: 25 minutes

1 small onion, finely chopped
½ bunch green onions, finely chopped
⅛ tsp. cinnamon
2–3 tsp. salt
¼ tsp. pepper
¾ cup cooked and cooled quinoa
2 large bunches of curly leaf parsley, finely chopped
2 large tomatoes, finely chopped
½–⅔ cup lemon juice
½ cup olive oil

1. In the bottom of a medium-sized mixing bowl, mix together the onion, green onions, cinnamon, salt, and pepper.

2. Add the remaining ingredients and toss together. Taste to be sure you have enough lemon juice and olive oil.

Tip:

I like to let this sit for a couple hours in the refrigerator before serving. The flavors really start to come together then!

Desserts

Snickers Apple Salad

Jennifer Archer
Kalona, IA

*Gluten-Free, Vegetarian

Makes 10–12 servings

Prep. Time: 15–20 minutes

3-oz. pkg. instant vanilla pudding

1 cup milk

8-oz. container frozen whipped topping, thawed

6 apples, peeled or unpeeled, diced

6 Snickers bars, diced or broken

1. Mix pudding with milk in a large mixing bowl.

2. Fold in whipped topping.

3. Fold in chopped apples and Snickers.

4. Cover and refrigerate until ready to serve.

Gluten-Free Pretzel Jello

Hope Comerford
Clinton Township, MI

*Gluten-Free, Vegetarian

Makes 12 servings

Prep. Time: 1 hour   ⚬   Bake Time: 10 minutes   ⚬   Chilling Time: 4 hours or until set

Crust:

3 cups crushed gluten-free pretzels

1½ sticks (12 Tbsp.) butter, melted

2 Tbsp. sugar

1 cup sugar

8 oz. cream cheese, softened

16 oz. frozen whipped topping, thawed

6-oz. pkg. strawberry gelatin

2 cups hot water

20 oz. frozen strawberries, thawed

1. Preheat the oven to 375°F.

2. Mix the crust ingredients and press them into a 9×13-inch baking pan. Bake for 10 minutes and let cool.

3. Mix the sugar and cream cheese. Gently fold in the topping. Spread this mixture over the cooled crust and refrigerate.

4. Mix the gelatin and water until dissolved. Add the strawberries and let cool a bit.

5. Spoon the gelatin mixture over the cream cheese mixture.

6. Refrigerate about 4 hours, or until completely set.

Peanut Butter Fudge

Jamie Schwankl
Ephrata, PA

*Gluten-Free, Vegetarian

Makes 16 servings

Prep. Time: 10 minutes ⚸ *Cooking Time: 5–8 minutes*

2 sticks (16 Tbsp.) butter or margarine
1 tsp. vanilla extract
1 cup peanut butter
pinch of salt
3 cups confectioners' sugar

1. Melt butter in a medium saucepan over low heat.

2. Add vanilla, peanut butter, and salt. Mix with a spoon until smooth. Remove from heat.

3. Add confectioners' sugar. Stir until well blended.

4. Spread mixture in an 8×8-inch pan to cool.

5. Refrigerate 1 hour. Cut into small squares.

Tips:

1. A 7×9-inch pan also works well.
2. Do not use a mixer.

Pecan Pie Squares

OVEN

Mary Ann Bowman
Ephrata, PA

Arianne Hochstetler
Goshen, IN

*Vegetarian

Makes 24 bars

Prep. Time: 15 minutes ⚓ *Baking Time: 35–40 minutes*

Crust:
1 ½ cups flour
3 Tbsp. brown sugar
¼ tsp. salt
1 stick (8 Tbsp.) butter

2 eggs
½ cup light corn syrup
½ cup brown sugar
1 cup chopped pecans
2 Tbsp. butter, melted
½ tsp. vanilla extract

1. Mix together flour, 3 Tbsp. brown sugar, and salt.

2. Cut butter into mixture with a pastry cutter or two knives until crumbly.

3. Press mixture into a greased 11×7-inch pan to form a crust.

4. Bake at 350°F for 15 minutes. Set aside, but do not turn off oven.

5. In a medium mixing bowl, beat eggs slightly.

6. Stir in corn syrup, ½ cup brown sugar, pecans, butter, and vanilla.

7. Pour over baked crust.

8. Put the pan back in the oven. Bake at 350°F for 20–25 minutes. Cool slightly. Cut into bars.

Lemon Squares

OVEN

Mary Kathryn Yoder
Harrisonville, MO

*Gluten-Free option, Vegetarian

Makes 15 servings

Prep. Time: 10 minutes ⚯ *Baking Time: 30 minutes* ⚯ *Cooling Time: 1–2 hours*

1 box angel food cake mix
21-oz. can lemon pie filling
⅛ cup confectioners' sugar

1. Mix cake mix and pie filling together with an electric mixer.

2. Pour into a lightly greased 9×13-inch baking pan.

3. Bake at 350°F for 30 minutes. Let cool.

4. Sprinkle confectioners' sugar over top.

5. Cut into bars.

*Recipe Note:

To make this recipe gluten-free, choose a gluten-free angel food cake mix and a gluten-free lemon pie filling.

Lemon Chocolate Chip Cookies

OVEN

Hope Comerford
Clinton Township, MI

Gluten-Free option, Vegetarian

Makes 24 cookies

Prep. Time: 10 minutes ⚶ Baking Time: 15 minutes

1 box lemon cake mix
2 eggs
½ cup vegetable oil or coconut oil
1 cup white chocolate chips

1. Preheat oven to 325°F.

2. Mix together the lemon cake mix, eggs, and vegetable oil. Stir in the white chocolate chips.

3. On a greased cookie sheet, or parchment paper lined cookie sheet, place 1½-tsp.-sized balls of dough 1 inch apart.

4. Bake for 15 minutes.

5. Let cool slightly, then place on a cooling rack.

*Recipe Note:

To make this recipe gluten-free, choose a gluten-free lemon cake mix, or use a gluten-free vanilla cake mix with 2 drops Young Living Essential Lemon Vitality Oil or 2 Tbsp. fresh lemon juice. Also, choose gluten-free white chocolate chips.

Chocolate Chip Cookies

Mary Martins
Fairbank, IA

*Vegetarian

Makes 3 dozen big cookies

Prep. Time: 15 minutes   Baking Time: 9 minutes per sheet   Chilling Time: 1 hour

2 sticks (16 Tbsp.) butter, at room temperature
1 cup brown sugar
1 cup sugar
3 eggs, beaten
3½ cups flour
2 tsp. cream of tartar
2 tsp. baking soda
½ tsp. salt
1 tsp. vanilla extract
12-oz. pkg. chocolate chips
1 cup chopped nuts, optional

1. In a large mixing bowl, combine butter, sugars, and eggs.

2. In a separate mixing bowl, sift together flour, cream of tartar, baking soda, and salt.

3. Add about one-third of the dry ingredients to the creamed mixture. Mix well. Add half of the remaining dry ingredients and mix well. Add the remaining dry ingredients and mix until thoroughly blended.

4. Stir in vanilla, chocolate chips, and nuts (if using). Chill in the fridge for 60 minutes.

5. Drop by spoonfuls onto a greased cookie sheet.

6. Bake at 400°F for about 9 minutes, or until lightly browned.

Tips:

1. If you like smaller cookies, make the spoonfuls in Step 5 about the size of a level teaspoon.

2. I usually bake a cookie sheet full and then cover the rest of the dough and keep it in the refrigerator for a day or so, so that I can have freshly baked cookies.

3. Use macadamia nuts in Step 4 for a real treat.

—Barb Yoder, Angola, IN

No-Bake Chocolate Cookies

Penny Blosser
Beavercreek, OH

Gluten-Free option, Vegetarian

Makes 36 cookies

Prep. Time: 20 minutes ⚶ *Cooking Time: 15 minutes* ⚶ *Cooling Time: 30 minutes*

½ cup tub margarine
½ cup milk
I cup Splenda Blend for Baking
I cup chocolate chips
½ cup peanut butter
I tsp. vanilla extract
3 cups quick oats

1. Put margarine, milk, Splenda, and chocolate chips in a saucepan.

2. Bring to boil, and boil 1 minute. Remove from heat.

3. Stir in peanut butter and vanilla until melted.

4. Add rolled oats. Mix.

5. Drop by heaping tablespoonfuls onto waxed paper–lined baking sheet.

6. Let cool until set.

*Recipe Note:

To make this recipe gluten-free, choose gluten-free chocolate chips and gluten-free quick oats.

Chocolate Trifle

Ruth E. Martin
Loysville, PA

*Gluten-Free option, Vegetarian

Makes 6–8 servings

Prep. Time: 15–20 minutes ⚬ *Cooking Time: 20 minutes* ⚬ *Chilling Time: 1 hour*

Chocolate Pudding:

1 egg yolk, slightly beaten

⅔ cup sugar

3 Tbsp. unsweetened cocoa powder

3 Tbsp. cornstarch

1½ cups milk

2 tsp. instant coffee granules

1 Tbsp. butter

½ tsp. vanilla extract

3 cups chocolate cake crumbs

12 oz. frozen whipped topping, thawed

½ cup Heath English Toffee Bits

*Recipe Note:

To make this recipe gluten-free, use gluten-free cake crumbs.

1. Put egg yolk in a medium bowl.

2. In medium saucepan, stir together sugar, cocoa, cornstarch, milk, and instant coffee.

3. Cook, stirring constantly, until mixture boils. Boil and stir 1 minute. Remove from heat.

4. Gradually stir small amount of hot mixture into egg yolk, whisking well.

5. Return to pan, stir and heat again until boiling. Remove from heat.

6. Stir in butter and vanilla. Lay plastic wrap directly on the surface. Chill at least one hour.

7. To assemble the trifle, in a clear glass bowl, put a third of the cake crumbs, then a third of the pudding, then a third of the whipped topping. Sprinkle with Heath bits. Repeat twice more, ending with Heath bits on top.

Cherry Cheesecake Tarts

Jan Mast
Lancaster, PA

Gluten-Free option, Vegetarian

Makes 18 servings

Prep. Time: 15 minutes ❧ Baking Time: 15–20 minutes

18 vanilla wafers
8-oz. cream cheese, softened
3 eggs
¾ cup sugar
21-oz. can cherry pie filling

*Recipe Note:
To make this recipe gluten-free, use gluten-free vanilla wafers and choose a gluten-free cherry pie filling.

1. Fill 18 cupcake tins with paper cupcake liners.

2. Place one vanilla wafer in each paper liner. Set aside.

3. Beat cream cheese just until soft and smooth. Do not overbeat.

4. Add eggs and sugar, beating until just blended. Do not overbeat.

5. Pour cream cheese mixture evenly into 18 cupcake liners, covering vanilla wafer.

6. Bake at 325°F degrees for 15–20 minutes. Cool completely.

7. Top each cooled tart with cherry pie filling.

Tips:

1. Use blueberry pie filling instead, or eliminate pie filling and use slices of assorted fresh fruits like kiwi, orange, strawberry, etc.

2. Refrigerate after preparing.

3. Do not overbeat the cream cheese mixture—it needs to be heavy enough to keep the wafers at the bottom. If too much air is beaten into it, the wafers will float to the top.

Dump Cake

Janie Steele
Moore, OK

Gluten-Free option, Vegetarian, Plant-Based option

Makes 8–10 servings

Prep. Time: 10 minutes ⚶ Cooking Time: 12 minutes ⚶ Setting: Manual
Pressure: High ⚶ Release: Manual

6 Tbsp. butter
1 box cake mix (I used spice)
2 (20-oz.) cans pie filling (I use apple)

1. Mix butter and dry cake mix in bowl. It will be clumpy.

2. Pour pie filling in the inner pot of the Instant Pot.

3. Pour the dry mix over top.

4. Secure lid and make sure vent is at sealing. Cook for 12 minutes on Manual mode at high pressure.

5. Release pressure manually when cook time is up and remove lid to prevent condensation from getting into cake.

6. Let stand 5–10 minutes.

*Recipe Notes:

To make this recipe gluten-free, choose a gluten-free cake mix and gluten-free pie filling.

To make this recipe plant-based, replace the butter with vegan butter or coconut oil.

Serving suggestion:
Serve with ice cream.

Chocolate Peanut Butter Swirl Dump Cake

SLOW-COOKER

Hope Comerford
Clinton Township, MI

*Gluten-Free option, Vegetarian

Makes 8–10 servings

Prep. Time: 10 minutes ⚜ *Cooking Time: 2–4 hours* ⚜ *Ideal slow-cooker size: 3½- to 4-qt.*

15¼-oz. box chocolate cake mix

3.4-oz. box butterscotch instant pudding

1¾ cups milk

4 1½-oz. pkgs. Reese's Peanut Butter Cups, chopped

¼ cup peanut butter

1. Spray crock with nonstick spray.

2. In a bowl, mix together the first three ingredients, then dump them into the crock.

3. Sprinkle chopped Reese's over the top of the batter, then swirl the peanut butter in with a spoon.

4. Cover and cook on Low for 2–4 hours.

*Recipe Note:
To make this recipe gluten-free, choose a gluten-free chocolate cake mix and gluten-free butterscotch instant pudding.

Blueberry Swirl Cake

Lori Lehman
Ephrata, PA

*Gluten-Free option, Vegetarian

Makes 15 servings

Prep. Time: 15 minutes ⚮ Baking Time: 30–40 minutes

3-oz. pkg. cream cheese, softened
18¼-oz. box white cake mix
3 eggs
3 Tbsp. water
21-oz. can blueberry pie filling

1. Beat cream cheese in a large mixing bowl until soft and creamy.

2. Stir in dry cake mix, eggs, and water. Blend well with cream cheese.

3. Pour into a greased 9×13-inch baking pan.

4. Pour blueberry pie filling over top of batter.

5. Swirl blueberries and batter with a knife by zigzagging through batter.

6. Bake at 350°F for 30–40 minutes, or until tester inserted in center comes out clean.

*Recipe Note:

To make this recipe gluten-free, choose a gluten-free cake mix and gluten-free blueberry pie filling.

Simply Apple Dump Cake

Hope Comerford
Clinton Township, MI

Gluten-Free option, Vegetarian, Plant-Based option

Make 10–12 servings

Prep. Time: 10 minutes ⚭ Cooking Time: 3–5 hours ⚭ Ideal slow-cooker size: 3½- or 4-qt.

21-oz. can apple pie filling
18¾-oz. box yellow cake mix
8 Tbsp. (1 stick) butter, melted

1. Spray crock with nonstick spray.

2. Dump apple pie filling into crock.

3. In a bowl, mix together the yellow cake mix and melted butter. Spoon this into the crock.

4. Cover and cook on Low for 3–5 hours.

*Recipe Notes:

To make this recipe gluten-free, choose gluten-free apple pie filling and gluten-free cake mix.

To make this recipe plant-based, replace the butter with vegan butter.

Peach Crisp

SLOW-COOKER

Janie Steele
Moore, OK

*Gluten-Free option, Vegetarian, Plant-Based

Makes 4–6 servings

Prep. Time: 20 minutes ⚸ *Cooking Time: 4–5 hours* ⚸ *Ideal slow-cooker size: 5-qt.*

¼ cup biscuit mix
⅔ cup quick or rolled oats
1½ tsp. cinnamon
¾ cup brown sugar
4 cups canned peaches, cut in chunks
½ cup peach juice

1. Mix biscuit mix, oats, cinnamon, and brown sugar in a bowl.

2. Place peaches and juice in bottom of greased slow cooker.

3. Add dry ingredients over top of peaches.

4. Stir slightly to gently coat peaches.

5. Cook on Low 3½–4½ hours covered, then remove lid for the last 30 minutes.

*Recipe Note:

To make this recipe gluten-free, choose a gluten-free baking mix instead of the biscuit mix and choose gluten-free oats.

Serving suggestion:

Serve with ice cream or whipped topping.

Cheesecake Bars

Leona Yoder
Hartville, OH

*Vegetarian

Makes 12 bars

Prep. Time: 10–15 minutes 🌿 *Baking Time: 40 minutes*

1 cup flour
⅓ cup brown sugar
⅓ cup (5⅓ Tbsp.) butter, melted
¼ cup sugar
1 large egg
1 Tbsp. lemon juice
2 Tbsp. milk
1 tsp. vanilla extract

1. Mix flour, brown sugar, and butter together in an electric mixing bowl. Reserve 1 cup mixture. Press remainder into a greased 8×8-inch baking pan.

2. Bake at 350°F for 15 minutes.

3. Meanwhile, in the mixing bowl, beat together the remaining ingredients. Spread on baked crust.

4. Top with reserved crumbs and bake for 25 minutes, or until set.

Extra Information

Abbreviations used in this cookbook

lb. = pound

oz. = ounce

pkg. = package

pt. = pint

qt. = quart

Tbsp. = tablespoon

tsp. = teaspoon

9 x 13 baking pan = 9 inches wide by 13 inches long

8 x 8 baking pan = 8 inches wide by 8 inches long

5 x 9 loaf pan = 5 inches wide by 9 inches long

Assumptions

flour = unbleached or white, and all-purpose

oatmeal or oats = dry, quick or rolled (old-fashioned),unless specified

pepper = black, finely ground

rice = regular, long-grain (not minute or instant)

salt = table salt

shortening = solid, not liquid

spices = all ground, unless specified otherwise

sugar = granulated sugar (not brown and not confectioners')

Equivalents

dash = little less than $\frac{1}{8}$ tsp.

3 teaspoons = 1 Tablespoon

2 Tablespoons = 1 oz.

4 Tablespoons = $\frac{1}{4}$ cup

5 Tablespoons plus 1 tsp. = $\frac{1}{3}$ cup

8 Tablespoons = $\frac{1}{2}$ cup

12 Tablespoons = $\frac{3}{4}$ cup

16 Tablespoons = 1 cup

1 cup = 8 oz. liquid

2 cups = 1 pint

4 cups = 1 quart

4 quarts = 1 gallon

1 stick butter = ¼ lb.

1 stick butter = ½ cup

1 stick butter = 8 Tbsp.

Beans, 1 lb. dried = 2–2½ cups (depending upon the size of the beans)

Bell peppers, 1 large = 1 cup chopped

Cheese, hard (for example, cheddar, Swiss, Monterey Jack, mozzarella), 1 lb. grated = 4 cups

Cheese, cottage, 1 lb. = 2 cups

Chocolate chips, 6-oz. pkg. = 1 scant cup

Coconut, 3-oz. pkg., grated = 1 cup, lightly filled

Crackers, graham, 12 single crackers = 1 cup crumbs

Crackers (butter, saltines, snack), 20 single crackers = 1 cup crumbs

Herbs, 1 Tbsp. fresh = 1 tsp. dried

Lemon, 1 medium-sized = 2–3 Tbsp. juice

Lemon, 1 medium-sized = 2–3 tsp. grated rind

Mustard, 1 Tbsp. prepared = 1 tsp. dry or ground mustard

Oatmeal, 1 lb. dry = about 5 cups dry

Onion, 1 medium-sized = ½ cup chopped

Pasta: Macaronis, penne, and other small or tubular shapes, 1 lb. dry = 4 cups uncooked

Noodles, 1 lb. dry = 6 cups uncooked spaghetti, linguine, fettucine, 1 lb. dry = 4 cups uncooked

Potatoes, white, 1 lb. = 3 medium-sized potatoes = 2 cups mashed

Potatoes, sweet, 1 lb. = 3 medium-sized potatoes = 2 cups mashed

Rice, 1 lb. dry = 2 cups uncooked

Sugar, confectioners', 1 lb. = 3½ cups sifted

Whipping cream, 1 cup un-whipped = 2 cups whipped

Whipped topping, 8-oz. container = 3 cups

Yeast, dry, 1 envelope (1/4 oz.) = 1 Tbsp.

Metric Equivalent Measurements

If you're accustomed to using metric measurements, I don't want you to be inconvenienced by the imperial measurements I use in this book.

Use this handy chart, too, to figure out the size of the slow cooker you'll need for each recipe.

Weight (Dry Ingredients)

1 oz		30 g
4 oz	¼ lb	120 g
8 oz	½ lb	240 g
12 oz	¾ lb	360 g
16 oz	1 lb	480 g
32 oz	2 lb	960 g

Slow Cooker Sizes

1-quart	0.96 l
2-quart	1.92 l
3-quart	2.88 l
4-quart	3.84 l
5-quart	4.80 l
6-quart	5.76 l
7-quart	6.72 l
8-quart	7.68 l

Volume (Liquid Ingredients)

½ tsp.		2 ml
1 tsp.		5 ml
1 Tbsp.	½ fl oz	15 ml
2 Tbsp.	1 fl oz	30 ml
¼ cup	2 fl oz	60 ml
⅓ cup	3 fl oz	80 ml
½ cup	4 fl oz	120 ml
⅔ cup	5 fl oz	160 ml
¾ cup	6 fl oz	180 ml
1 cup	8 fl oz	240 ml
1 pt	16 fl oz	480 ml
1 qt	32 fl oz	960 ml

Length

¼ in	6 mm
½ in	13 mm
¾ in	19 mm
1 in	25 mm
6 in	15 cm
12 in	30 cm

Special Diet Index

Index

About the Author

Hope Comerford is a mom, wife, elementary music teacher, blogger, recipe developer, public speaker, Young Living Essential Oils essential oil enthusiast/educator, and published author. In 2013, she was diagnosed with a severe gluten intolerance and since then has spent many hours creating easy, practical and delicious gluten-free recipes that can be enjoyed by both those who are affected by gluten and those who are not.

Growing up, Hope spent many hours in the kitchen with her Meme (grandmother) and her love for cooking grew from there. While working on her master's degree when her daughter was young, Hope turned to her slow cookers for some salvation and sanity. It was from there she began truly experimenting with recipes and quickly learned she had the ability to get a little more creative in the kitchen and develop her own recipes.

In 2010, Hope started her blog, A Busy Mom's Slow Cooker Adventures, to simply share the recipes she was making with her family and friends. She never imagined people all over the world would begin visiting her page and sharing her recipes with others as well. In 2013, Hope self-published her first cookbook, *Slow Cooker Recipes 10 Ingredients or Less and Gluten-Free*, and then later wrote *The Gluten-Free Slow Cooker*.

Hope became the new brand ambassador and author of Fix-It and Forget-It in mid-2016. Since then, she has brought her excitement and creativeness to the Fix-It and Forget-It brand. Through Fix-It and Forget-It, she has written *Fix-It and Forget-It Lazy & Slow, Fix-It and Forget-It Healthy Slow Cooker Cookbook, Fix-It and Forget-It Cooking for Two, Fix-It and Forget-It Instant Pot Cookbook, Fix-It and Forget-It Freezer Meals, Welcome Home Cookbook*, and many more.

Hope lives in the city of Clinton Township, Michigan, near Metro Detroit. She has been happily married to her husband and best friend, Justin, since 2008. Together they have two children, Ella and Gavin, who are her motivation, inspiration, and heart. In her spare time, Hope enjoys traveling, singing, cooking, reading books, spending time with friends and family, and relaxing.